Advance praise for *Whistle Posts West*

"This book helped me relive train trips through the Rockies and across the Prairies as an eight-summer CPR dining-car pantry-man and waiter in the 1960s... Terrific stories about the lure and impact of railroading in Canada [told with] punchy, robust writing."
MIKE HARCOURT former premier of BC and former railroader

"Capturing the environment of railroading and putting it on paper embeds the reader in the dedication of these writers. The detail and perspective in their writing are refreshing. This book will become a classic."
HERB DIXON president, Alberta Railway Museum

"*Whistle Posts West* is a must-read for serious train buffs and armchair rail travellers alike. It has tragedy, intrigue, humour, poetry, and railroad jargon (learn about hoggers, buzzard's roost, deadman's throttle, and beanery queens). It is especially rich with Western Canadian history... so sit back and enjoy the ride!"
GARRY MARCHANT author of *The Peace Correspondent*

"North America's toughest railroading imaginable, its grandest gold rush, and its most fascinating legends all happened in this northwestern corner of the continent. The authors bring their train tales alive through striking incidents, surprising anecdotes, and wonderful writing. This book is fun and frightening; it's sad, fierce, and hilarious. Here you have a treasure trove of history—some larger-than-life accounts, some rather small happenings. Read *Whistle Posts West* and jump aboard Canada's love affair with trains."
DON WAITE author of *British Columbia and Yukon Gold Hunters*

"I wish to congratulate Mary Trainer, Brian Antonson, and Rick Antonson on their fine job. Their work and research will trigger many memories in the minds of those of us with a railroad background. Canadian railroading has been a treasured way of life for many who have viewed [the country] from a train locomotive cab or caboose or worked on the track or in the roundhouses, freight sheds, stations, car shops, offices, and outpost assignments. Canadians and people from other nations will find *Whistle Posts West* a great read.

My experience on the railroad began in 1940 at Hanna, Alberta, when I was seven years old and my Dad, Jack Home, gave me a ride on the 2021 steam locomotive. I've been hooked on railroading ever since!"

HARRY HOME member, Canadian Railway Hall of Fame

"A treasure trove of train stories, though I admit to a favourite. What a great combination: poet Robert Service and the White Pass and Yukon Railway, both internationally renowned for their northern spirit of adventure. *Whistle Posts West* blends the two for a fun and informative read. Today, the narrow-gauged WP&YR, Canada's most westerly set of rails, still lures thrill seekers north to experience its steep grades and sheer canyon walls."

THE HONOURABLE IONE J. CHRISTENSEN former senator from Yukon; member, Order of Canada; author of *Life at the Edge*

Praise for *Slumach's Gold: In Search of a Legend*

"Qualifies as a British Columbia classic." BC *BookWorld*

"A great piece of research that reads like a mystery novel or a CSI episode ... *Slumach's Gold* combines legend, myth, documentation, and oral history. It's a masterpiece."
RICHARD THOMAS WRIGHT author of *Barkerville and the Cariboo Goldfields*

"A fresh new look at one of British Columbia's enduring mysteries."
CHUCK DAVIS author of *The Chuck Davis History of Metropolitan Vancouver*

"A wonderful mythology about untold riches hidden in the mountains around British Columbia's Pitt Lake. A vital source of information for armchair dreamers and true prospectors alike."
FRED BRACHES Slumach.ca

Fort Steele: A steam train takes you back a hundred years.
FORT STEELE HERITAGE TOWN

Mary Trainer, Brian Antonson, and Rick Antonson

WHISTLE POSTS WEST

Railway Tales from
British Columbia, Alberta, and Yukon

VICTORIA • VANCOUVER • CALGARY

BRIAN ANTONSON

You see them alongside train tracks across North America—
posts bearing white signs with one simple letter: "W."
They're "whistle posts," a reminder to engineers to sound
their train horns before entering a crossing.

Heritage House Publishing Company Ltd.
heritagehouse.ca

Cataloguing Information available from Library and Archives Canada

978-1-77203-043-3 (pbk)
978-1-77203-044-0 (epub)
978-1-77203-045-7 (epdf)

Edited by Karla Decker
Proofread by Lara Kordic
Cover design by Jacqui Thomas
Interior design by Setareh Ashrafologhalai
Map by Eric Leinberger,
    Leinberger Mapping

Cover images: "CP 2816 under Full Steam," Revelstoke, BC (front); "Rocky Mountaineer by moonlight," Robert Bittner, photographer, revybawb70@me.com (back)
Rocky Mountaineer™ is a trademark of the Great Canadian Railtour Company Ltd.

The following stories are reproduced with the permission of their respective authors: "A Day Out of the Ordinary," by Bruce Harvey (2015); "Leaving Town," by Clif Chapman (2015); "Miracle below Savona," by Joe Smuin (2013).

Disclaimer: While every effort has been taken to ensure accuracy, any errors that appear are the responsibility of the authors. We are enthusiastic about trains and railways yet respect there is a world of railroaders for whom specifics and details are a fact of daily life, and we defer to their readings for any updates, revisions, or clarifications we should make in future editions of this book.

The interior of this book was produced on 100% post-consumer recycled paper, processed chlorine free and printed with vegetable-based inks.

Heritage House acknowledges the financial support for its publishing program from the Government of Canada through the Canada Book Fund (CBF), Canada Council for the Arts, and the Province of British Columbia through the British Columbia Arts Council and the Book Publishing Tax Credit.

19 18 17 16 15   1 2 3 4 5

Printed in Canada

*To steam whistles that once drifted across the
Canadian prairie and echoed in far-off hills;*

*To diesel horns that beckon today, calling our hearts
to tracks and trestles everywhere—a wistful,
comforting reminder of times past;*

*And to heritage keepers,
who share our love of trains.*

AUTHORS' NOTE

WHILE RAILROADS, AIRLINES, and the military commonly use the twenty-four-hour clock, because North Americans are more familiar with the twelve-hour clock, we have chosen to use it in our book. Sandford Fleming, a CPR director and railway engineer who surveyed the first railroad route across the country, also established an international standard time system.

BRIAN ANTONSON

CONTENTS

FOREWORD

IF THERE IS one thing I have learned while spending more than forty years in the field of railway preservation, it is that everyone seems to have a train story. Whether it is from a time long ago, perhaps recalled by a relative who has a past linked to the railway, or from someone who loves to watch or ride a train, the stories emerge. Whenever I speak with people at our railway heritage facility, I am intrigued by the new and seemingly endless tales that unfold.

Trains have made an impact on all of us in many ways. Whether it is because they seem so large and powerful, or whether memories of a special or particularly enchanting trip are rekindled, a passing train gives pause for a look, a turn away from the current bustle.

This book has captures some compelling stories that illustrate why and how the railways continue to spark our imaginations. From the 1880s to today, from tragedy to high drama, from the humorous to the absurd, *Whistle Posts West* will engage you to the finish.

I took my first train journey in 1955 aboard Canadian Pacific's brand-new Canadian. It started a lifelong passion for railways that has led to years of work in railway preservation, including the creation of the West Coast Railway Heritage Park in Squamish, BC, and many years on the board of the Association of Tourist Railways and Railway Museums. My wife and I love to travel, and to this day we never take a trip that doesn't have a rail journey in the itinerary.

So, climb on board and enjoy some great railway stories!

DON EVANS, President Emeritus, West Coast Railway Association

Passenger rail experiences are thriving in Western Canada, and the two most widely experienced are operated by the independently owned Rocky Mountaineer and the federal crown corporation VIA Rail (shown here). **VIA RAIL CANADA**

INTRODUCTION

OUR SHARED PASSION for trains began in the 1950s—long before we co-authored works about Western Canada's history. As children, we grew up with the echoes of distant steam-train whistles and, later, diesel horns. How well we remember the puffs of smoke emanating from locomotives chugging along the Kettle Valley Railway high up into the dry Okanagan hills. Or the unforgettable experience of standing in awe alongside a huge F unit locomotive!

There were family trips by train too, where lasting impressions of the magnificent Canadian landscape were created—like the grand spectacle of the Rocky Mountains or the endless fields of prairie wheat waving in a summer breeze.

We recall seeing, as young adults, a lifeless but stately Royal Hudson 2860 awaiting restoration; it would become wonderfully revitalized under steam. We've cycled along abandoned railbeds, travelled many of the world's most exotic railways, and supported efforts to preserve and promote our railway heritage.

Today, like rail fans everywhere, we're thrilled to stop at a crossing to admire modern consists thundering by, sometimes several kilometres long. As drivers alongside a moving train, we occasionally pull over to recapture a winsome childhood memory and, yes, to wave at crew and passengers. And when the opportunity arises to travel by train, we take it.

And so we embraced the opportunity to create this work with great enthusiasm. Herein, you'll find stories that span a century and a half, that cover the plains and foothills of Alberta, the mountains and valleys of British Columbia, and treacherous territory in Yukon. They recount disasters and near disasters, the business of the routes and rails, the realities of working on the railroads, and rollicking good stories that paint a panorama stretching from the sublime to the ridiculous.

Rails may speak to us, but they're simply mute ribbons of steel until they become a railroad. Once a locomotive moves down the line with a train in tow, the rails positively sing!

"What's past is prologue," wrote Shakespeare. Sadly, he never had the privilege of writing about these rails. Happily, we have, and the journey has been so very satisfying.

Perhaps most rewarding in researching and writing this book has been the joy of connecting with long-time, passionate railroaders who know first-hand—far better than we—the excitement, hard work, and commitment it takes to bind our country by rail.

MARY TRAINER, BRIAN ANTONSON, AND RICK ANTONSON

A VIA Rail train works its way through the magnificent Rockies with passengers from around the world. VIA RAIL CANADA

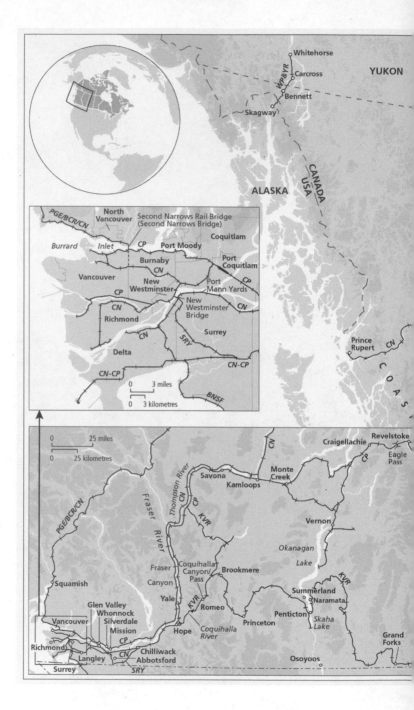

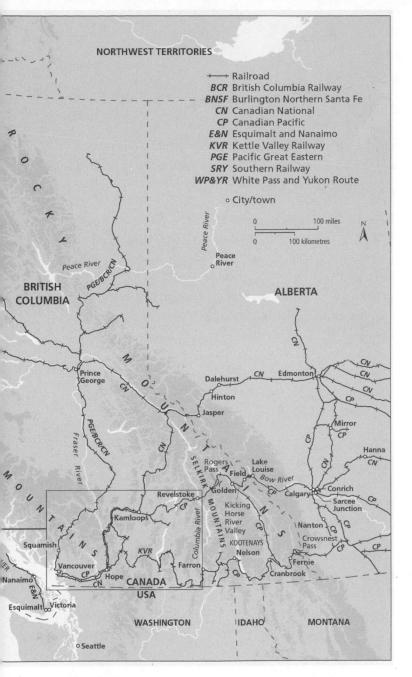

TIME TUNNEL

THE STORIES IN this book unfold in the context of many other events in railroad history and Canadian history in general. Our story titles are included here in *italics*.

1793 Alexander Mackenzie becomes the first explorer to cross North America to the Pacific Ocean, predating Lewis and Clark's expedition by a decade.

1818 The Canada–United States border is designated as the 49th parallel from the Pacific Ocean eastward to Manitoba/Minnesota.

1836 Canada's first publicly accessible train begins running, pulled by the "Dorchester" for the Champlain and St. Lawrence Railroad near Montreal.

1857 The Fraser River and Cariboo Gold Rushes in British Columbia begin.

1858 The Colony of British Columbia is established, with New Westminster becoming its capital in 1859.

1863 The Vancouver Coal Mining Company begins as Western Canada's first railway, near Nanaimo.

1867 Canadian Confederation forms the Dominion of Canada.

1869 Union Pacific and Central Pacific locomotives meet at Promontory Summit, and the US's "last spike" is driven, forming North America's first transcontinental railroad.

1871 British Columbia joins Confederation.

1872 Kicking Horse Pass, BC, becomes part of the Canadian Pacific Railway.

1873 Yellowhead Pass, BC, becomes part of the CPR.
- *Pathways to the West: Finding Rail Routes through the Rockies*
- *Promises, Promises*

1879 The Government of Canada forms the Department of Railways and Canals.

1881 Rogers Pass forms part of the CPR.
- *Pathways to the West: Finding Rail Routes through the Rockies*

1881–84
- *From China to the Rails of Gold Mountain*

1883 Incorporation of the Esquimalt and Nanaimo Railway (E&N). The first transcontinental train arrives in Calgary.

1885 Troops transported via CPR trains to quell the Northwest Rebellion, led by Louis Riel, demonstrate the viability of the national dream, leading to its completion across the Prairies.
- *The Craigellachie Kid and the Four "Last Spikes"*

1886
- *Women at Work—and Play—on the Railroad*

1887 The first CPR train arrives in Vancouver.

1889 The CPR completes its "coast-to-coast" connection.

LATE 1880S–1930S High-speed silk trains operate across North America.
- *As Smooth as Silk*

1896 The Klondike Gold Rush begins.
- *A Buckling Tragedy at Point Ellice*

1898 The Yukon splits from the Northwest Territories to form Yukon Territory, now Yukon.

1900 The White Pass and Yukon Route Railway begins service.

1904
- *Billy Miner's Missing Loot*
- *Poetry in Locomotion: Yukon's Bard Arrives by Train*

1905 Alberta joins Confederation.

1906
- *Sunken Engine Creek*

1907
- *"This Is a Holdup. Give Us Your Coal!"*

1910 Interurban service begins between New Westminster and Chilliwack, ending in the 1950s.

1914 First World War commences and involves much rail movement of armed forces, equipment, and supplies.

1914–15
- *Building the Kettle Valley Railroad: A Boy's-eye View*

1915 The Kettle Valley Line's first passenger service is established between Midway and Merritt.

1919 The Canadian National Railway is incorporated.

1924
- *Terrorism on the Tracks*

1926
- *Hard Luck Locomotive Number One*

1935
- *Romeo's Snow Slide*

1939 The Second World War begins and spurs even more rail movement of armed forces, equipment, and supplies. CPR Hudson locomotives receive the "Royal Hudson" designation from King George VI.
- *A Royal Locomotive Rides the Rails*

1940S
- *Whistling Up a Warning*

1943
- *Women at Work—and Play—on the Railroad*

LATE 1940S
- *Delectable Derailment*

1947
- *Caboose on the Loose*

1949
- *One Hell of a Roar*

1950s

- *Terrorism on the Tracks*

1953

- *Leaving Town*

1956

- *Hard Luck Locomotive Number Two*

1960 The era of steam ends for the CNR, then the CPR.

1967

- *Hard Luck Locomotive Number Three*

1968 The Alberta Railway Museum opens.

1969

- *The Train with No Name*

1974–99 The refurbished Royal Hudson steam locomotive runs between Squamish and North Vancouver.

1975

- *Miracle below Savona*

1977 VIA Rail is incorporated.

1981

- *Railway Ruse*

1982

- *A Day out of the Ordinary*

1986 Steam Expo occurs in Vancouver as part of Expo '86.
- *Eighteen Seconds to Hell*

1988
- *The Mountaineer*

1994 The Westcoast Railway Heritage Park opens in Squamish.

1999
- *Bridges and Barges Don't Mix Well*

2002
- *A National Icon Comes Aboard*

2003
- *Which Piece Goes Where?*

2007
- *Women at Work—and Play—on the Railroad*

THE FUTURE
- *Interurbanation*

ROUTES AND RAILS

CANADA BECAME a country on July 1, 1867. But what really united the nation was the building of the transcontinental railroad during the late 1880s. In this section, we read of the explorers and entrepreneurs who worked at finding viable routes across dramatic obstacles like the Rocky Mountains, and those whose sweat and blood made those routes a reality. Then there were the trades and businesses that benefitted from the transcontinental connection, one being the high-speed silk trains that bolted through the countryside until the 1930s with their precious cargo of silk in the making. Finally, we get a glimpse into the story behind the new railway line that brought Robert Service, the renowned "Bard of the Yukon," to this place that so inspired him.

◄ Fort Edmonton's 1919 Baldwin Steam Train brings you to the Hudson's Bay Fort's 1846 station. **FORT EDMONTON PARK**

PATHWAYS TO THE WEST
Finding Rail Routes through the Rockies

BEFORE THE MOUNTAIN reaches echoed with the sounds of the railroad and plumes of smoke and steam rose up to the sky, adventurous souls had come quietly, with their maps, compasses, and dreams.

The earliest Europeans to see this land were explorers, including Alexander Mackenzie, Simon Fraser, David Thompson, and John Palliser. Later came the men working for the railroad, on foot and horseback, men named Moberly, Macoun, and Rogers, leading their teams of surveyors who would probe canyons, valleys, and passes, finding routes for the rails that would follow.

The West was largely uncharted then; huge swaths of today's Western Canada were untracked wilderness, known only to the First Nations that had called this region home for millennia.

The surveyors came with a mission: to find routes for the rails that would open up the land and establish the promised connection for the young nation of Canada. The country was formally established in 1867, with BC joining Confederation in 1871, in large part reacting to a promise made by Prime Minister John A. Macdonald that a railroad would be built. The region's gold-rush economy of a decade earlier had come to an end, and joining Canada held the promise of increased wealth for the West, even though the makeup of the country was still evolving. The concept of Prairie provinces, for example, was still years away: Manitoba had joined Confederation before BC, but it would take more than three decades for provinces of Alberta and Saskatchewan to be formed and enter Confederation, fulfilling the *A Mari Usque ad Mare* ("From sea to sea") motto of the new nation.

The passage of the rails through the grasslands and the foothills of the Rockies was fairly straightforward; surveyors could see the route ahead easily, and the horizon was flat and featureless. But then the Rockies and the Selkirk Mountains loomed, posing a huge problem: how could routes be forged through these daunting ranges to the Pacific—routes with manageable grades for the trains, and ones that a railway company could afford? Was the technology up to overcoming nature's challenges? And what of the obstacles presented by the Fraser and Thompson River canyons?

Walter Moberly was a surveyor and civil engineer by trade. He had worked in the West in the 1860s, surveying land for streets in New Westminster, and with Edgar Dewdney on the Dewdney Trail, which stretched across southwestern BC. He had also been involved with a company assigned to construct a portion of the Fraser Canyon Wagon Road.

In 1865, Moberly was the assistant surveyor general for the Colony of British Columbia. This role took him across the expanse of the province-to-be and eventually into the territory between Shuswap Lake and Revelstoke, where he discovered what later would be known as Eagle Pass, in the Monashee Mountains. Legend has it that he had shot at some eagles that then flew off up a valley; his shots had evidently missed their targets. He followed the eagles up the valley and found the pass he believed could one day be the route for a railway line from the East. Moberly wrote that he blazed a tree in the pass and inscribed the words, "This is the Pass of the Overland Railway." That prediction would not come true for two decades, but his foresight would prove remarkably accurate.

When BC joined Confederation, Moberly, invited by the new province's first lieutenant-governor, Joseph Trutch, began his surveying work for the Canadian Pacific Railway (CPR). But while he felt the Eagle Pass route he had found years earlier was the correct one, the CPR's chief engineer, Sandford Fleming, had different ideas: he wanted Moberly and his crews to follow a more northerly route through the Yellowhead Pass, which crosses the Continental Divide and straddles today's BC–Alberta border. Frustrated, Moberly quit the project in 1873, though the crews continued their work. In Ottawa, scandals relating to the railway expansion saw Prime Minister Macdonald's Conservative government voted out of office, but the search for routes across the mountains continued.

Botanist John Macoun came into the picture following a chance meeting in 1872 with Sandford Fleming. Bringing with him a determination to succeed, he worked on pushing a route through the future provinces of Saskatchewan and Alberta, thus firming up a southern route to where the rails entered the Rockies through the Kicking Horse Pass. The political advantage of a southern route occupying land closer to the American border was not lost on observers. With five forays under his leadership completed, Macoun moved to Ottawa to continue work on his first love, botany.

Major Albert Bowman Rogers came late to the game, joining the CPR's team in 1881, a full decade after the work to connect to the West began. Rogers had cut his teeth in the US, where he'd gained the sobriquet "The Railway Pathfinder." He took up the earlier work done by Moberly in 1865 and identified a route through BC's Selkirk range that led from the Columbia River up the Illecillewaet River, a route known today as Rogers Pass, which carries both the CPR main line and the Trans-Canada Highway. His crews faced the usual challenges of survival in the mountains, with food scarce and the work hard. Many resented his stern ways of leadership, with one observer noting that "his driving ambition was to have his name handed down in history"—a goal that would one day be achieved.

The crews pressed ahead nonetheless, and in the summer of 1882, the pass Rogers had seen the year before opened up before him, and the route forward was confirmed. He received the $5,000 cheque he had been promised by the CPR, and rather than cash it immediately he slipped it into a frame for all to see; it was a significant sum in those days. Another promise was kept, as well: the pass was named Rogers Pass in his honour. Other names from the CPR route such as Kicking Horse Pass, Field, and Golden entered the Canadian lexicon.

With the route now in place, work on the main line continued and was completed in 1885. By then, the route had moved south again, and now followed through Moberly's Eagle Pass, which became the place where the "Last Spike" was driven, at Craigellachie, an event that Rogers attended. Moberly was ever bitter with Rogers over this, maintaining that his earlier work had shown the way for his eventual successor. He felt he and his team members deserved recognition and naming rights, but that was not to be.

The work of men who found the rail routes was replaced by the efforts of those who toiled day and night to actually build the dream. The majority were European or Chinese, working for low wages in a high-stakes game. The mountain passes were dangerous places, and many died during the construction phase. No one named passes after them, and many remained completely anonymous in death as well. When their work was done, the thousands who had survived the ordeal were simply "released." Most of the Chinese workers were unable to afford to return to China and stayed in Canada to found new communities.

Those who had led the searches for routes went on to other things. Moberly moved to Manitoba, where he continued to work as a surveyor. Macoun gained the lofty title of "Explorer of the Northwest Territories" for his later work and became noted for his botanical enterprises; many of his field specimens are today in Ottawa's

Canadian Museum of Nature. Rogers continued his work south of the border, scouting out routes for the Great Northern Railway; a second pass is named for him in Montana.

The lives of these three men and their crews are forever linked with the rails that drew Canada together. Every metre of steel rail, every spike, every tie, every piece of gravel, every tunnel, every trestle and bridge follows the course plotted and built by these hardy men who experienced daily danger, privation, frequent disappointment as possible routes failed, weather problems, and separation from their families for weeks, months, or years. We owe them our deepest gratitude.

FROM CHINA TO THE
RAILS OF GOLD MOUNTAIN

WE CAN ONLY imagine what was going through their minds as they saw these forested shores for the first time. They'd come across the Pacific from China, travelling for weeks on often torturous voyages, leaving behind their crowded homeland and their families and friends, many of whom were mired in poverty.

In Canada, they sought hope. The endless green of the mountains and the deep grey of the inland waters would form their first impressions of this new land. An appreciation of its vastness would come soon enough.

They weren't the first Chinese people to venture to the west coast of North America. In their home provinces of Guangdong and Fujian, they called this new land "Gold Mountain." Many before them had come across the ocean to seek their fortunes in the California Gold Rush of 1848 and then the Fraser River and Cariboo Gold Rushes a decade later. But this time, it was different. The gold they sought would come from their work on the building of a railroad—or so they hoped.

Work on the transcontinental railroad in BC began thirteen years after Confederation. Thousands of workers would be needed to build the railroad up treacherous river canyons and over difficult mountain passes, a far greater labour supply than the young province could provide. And so eyes turned to Asia, and soon the people came, seeking their fortunes, futures, and money to help their families, which they had to leave behind. Others came north from the US, many having worked on the construction of American railroads. Estimates vary, but perhaps as many as 17,000 Chinese workers toiled on the Canadian Pacific Railway for more than half a decade.

Andrew Onderdonk was the enterprising engineer who brought many Chinese labourers to these shores. With contracts in hand to oversee construction from Port Moody to Craigellachie, Onderdonk mustered his workforce. Sadly, discrimination was rife in those days, and Chinese workers were paid much less than white people: a dollar a day was the going rate for the Chinese, whereas Caucasians received up to double that. The low wages paid Chinese workers are estimated to have reduced the cost of building the CPR by up to 25 percent, saving up to $5 million.

They were housed in tent camps, some with a thousand in each, and were required to pay for their room and board. They had to buy their own supplies at the company store, at inflated prices, and if they did not, they received a lower pay rate. Many white workers believed the Chinese immigrants were coming to steal jobs from Canadians. Clashes erupted, and suffering through the daily discrimination was intense.

Working on the railroad was difficult and dangerous as they cleared rights-of-way, built bridges, dug tunnels, prepared the roadbed, laid down almost a million ties, and constructed a wide variety of facilities along the route. Perhaps as many as two thousand Chinese workers died in accidents along the line, in explosions as dynamite cleared rock for tunnels and cuts, or of a variety of illnesses. Many died of scurvy due to a simple deficiency of vitamin C in their food. Because they were hired as "gangs" rather than as individuals, keeping track of how many came and how many died were huge challenges. A "bookman" hired by a contractor acted as a translator and kept track of individual hours, but anonymity was common.

Physical abuse was the norm. Contractors forced Chinese labourers to work more quickly, frequently beating them and spraying them with water spewed from hoses. Their diet was meagre. There were work stoppages and strikes protesting abuses, work conditions, and what the Chinese workers perceived to be unfair taxation. (They did, in fact, have to pay higher taxes than other workers.) Pay was stopped when winter fell and work became impossible. Family members living in China were seldom notified when their loved ones died. The workers found themselves in situations far different from their original dreams of success in Gold Mountain.

Some enterprising Chinese people were able to become merchants in this morass that was their new world. They became suppliers to both the Chinese population in the camps and to others working on the railroad. In some cases, individual enterprises grew to have several outlets.

Then, when it was all over and the last spike had been driven in November of 1885, the work for the most part was gone, and thousands were left with nothing to do and no place to go. Their wages often hadn't covered their expenses, so the concept of returning home to family and friends in China wasn't to be entertained. "Chinatowns" grew in the larger cities of BC, including Victoria, New Westminster, and Vancouver. A small number of Chinese workers settled in Revelstoke, and other communities along the line saw populations grow. Still others headed east, establishing themselves in Alberta or farther beyond, contributing to the growth of Chinese populations in those places.

Chinatowns were collections of narrow streets of shops, rooming houses, and early businesses such as Chinese laundries. "Benevolent associations" grew to provide a sense of community and help newcomers to these cities find their way.

Troubles continued, even multiplied, for the Chinese population when the construction of the railroad ended. Legislation denied them the right to vote. A head tax was instituted to slow down immigration. Economic and social acceptance was a goal that simply could not be achieved for many in those times.

Today, Western Canada's cities boast many Chinese citizens. It would be more than a century before moves attempting to redress wrongs done to Chinese Canadians would be made. The federal and provincial governments have both issued formal apologies, but few Chinese Canadians received compensation, and concern about the adequacy of these gestures continues to be a topic of national discussion. The fallout from the building of the national dream continues thirteen decades later.

THE CRAIGELLACHIE KID
AND THE FOUR "LAST SPIKES"

NOVEMBER 7, 1885. High in the Canadian Rockies, at a railway station named Craigellachie, near the summit of Eagle Pass, a large crowd of men gathered to witness CPR director Sir Donald Smith (later Lord Strathcona) drive the ceremonial last spike into the tracks that would connect Canada by rail. Within an hour, the assembled crowd would hear a conductor shout, "All aboard for the Pacific!" as the train chugged across the newly secured rails, gaining speed as it headed for Port Moody on the country's west coast, the first train to do so.

As Smith hammered home a five-inch spike that delivered on the young country's shared ambition to be joined by rail that morning in Eagle Pass, photographer Alexander Ross captured the occasion for posterity on his camera. Among the many shown looking on the scene with stern gazes in his photo are Sandford Fleming (a CPR director and railway engineer who surveyed this first railroad route across the country, and also established an international standard time system), and William Van Horne (then general manager and subsequently the second president of the CPR).

Historian Omer Lavallée later called this "Canada's most famous photograph." Often referred to as "The Last Spike," the picture shows fiercely determined, talented, and brave men of their time: rail workers, stonecutters, dynamiters, engineers, and bridge builders, along with dignitaries, investors, and visionaries. And amid the throng of big, rugged men stands a fresh-faced eighteen-year-old,

Edward Mallandaine. In *Towards the Last Spike*, poet E.J. Pratt wrote of him: "A water-boy had wormed his way in front, To touch this last rail with his foot."

Who was Mallandaine, and how did this young man find his way to this remote and intimidating neck of the woods? The truth is, he planned it that way. For some time, the teenager had been riding a pony between Farwell (today's Revelstoke) and the work camps near Eagle Pass, delivering whatever the workers had ordered—everything from newspapers to groceries, supplies, and water. In return, he would take away their mail and his fee. He'd even picked up a nickname, based on his youthful looks: the Craigellachie Kid.

As early as 1851, the British government had assured the colonies and provinces that British North America, as it was then named, would be linked by the Intercolonial Railway. But some envisioned an even greater stretch of steel. Statesman and poet Joseph Howe, speaking to a group in Nova Scotia, said "I believe that many in this room will live to hear the whistle of the steam engine in the passes of the Rocky Mountains and to make the journey from Halifax to the Pacific in five or six days."

British Columbia reluctantly joined the Dominion of Canada as a province in 1871, based on a promise that such a railroad would be built to connect it with Eastern Canada, three thousand miles and a handful of seemingly insurmountable mountain ranges away. Politically, this pact pre-empted growing separatist voices proposing that BC should forsake its British heritage and become part of the adjoining US, with which it shared active trade. Against all odds of weather, geography, politics, and finances, the virtually impossible railroad would eventually carve out a country all its own. Building the line would be called "the greatest adventure in railway history" and be unsurpassed for its engineering feats by any other country of the times.

An American, Andrew Onderdonk, was hired by the federal government to build the railway eastward through BC into the mountains, with the eventual mandate to meet the westbound CPR work crew at Eagle Pass. Perhaps seven thousand men of working age lived west of Ontario, too few for the job at hand. Onderdonk's onerous task was accomplished in part by his bringing in thousands of workers from China, many of whom were assigned the most dangerous tasks, worked the longest hours, and struggled against the harsh, foreign climate. A significant number of them were among the 8,002 individuals killed during the construction work, falling from canyon cliff sides, or being hit by exploded granite, or through exhaustion. One may wonder why they are not seen in the last spike photograph; the answer is that they were working on sections much farther west of Craigellachie.

Men of many nationalities built the railway. Scotsman George Stephen, later president of CPR, and financier Donald Smith, also Scottish, were cousins. During financial struggles that threatened the very existence of the railroad, and the profitable prospects of Canada's trade with Asia, these two men came to the fore in order to save the vision. Their pledge to personally close the company's financing gap was astounding as much for the positive repercussions as for the risk of ruin they each accepted. It is why they have been called "Empire Builders." In those darkest of times, Stephen sent his cousin and fellow CPR directors a coded cablegram from London that read: "Stand fast, Craigellachie!" (More correctly written as *Craig Ellachie*, the Gaelic term was the Clan Grant's war cry, which Stephen and Smith knew from when they were boys in their home country). Upon reading that emboldening cable from Stephen, Van Horne immediately chose the name for the yet-to-be-determined location where the Transcontinental's last rails would be laid and its completing spike driven.

Edward Mallandaine's presence at the historic occasion had been planned, too, though his plan to attend was not nearly as long in the making. The night before, he had hopped aboard a flatbed heading out of Farwell, travelling unprotected from a crushing cold and the rail car's cargo of steel as it moved toward Craigellachie. Mallandaine was determined to put his mark on this occasion just by attending. Among the few young white people to ever be in these mountains, he jostled with workers and dignitaries in order to get a preferred view of the historic proceedings.

Railway workers in those days were big, hearty, tough, and almost certainly bearded and messy. Youthful and smooth-skinned, Edward stood out. Having been born the day Canada became a country, on July 1, 1867, the lad seemed prescient about destiny. And he used his relative shortness as an excuse to get to the unfolding scene. In an article in *The Globe and Mail* of October 11, 2010, Neil Reynolds cites from Ray Argyle's book *The Craigellachie Kid*, a much older Mallandaine's memory of what happened next.

> "Can I get in?" he asked, moving closer to the action.
>
> "Whadda yuh doin' here?" someone shouted. "Get away, kid."
>
> "Let him in," one of the railway managers shouted. "Don't you know that's the Craigellachie Kid?"
>
> Moments later, Edward Mallandaine made history.

Despite the cold, Sir Donald Smith took off his overcoat to give himself more freedom to swing the heavy hammer. He passed it to an aide and took up his position, eyes firmly on the iron spike inserted into the track, just enough to keep it steady. As onlookers hushed, he aimed. Smith's first downward swing glanced off the spike, bending the iron head. The twisted metal piece was removed, tossed aside, and replaced with a handy spare. Smith, now the wiser,

On November 7, 1885, photographer Alexander Ross captured financier Donald Smith driving home the "last spike" to ceremonially complete the transcontinental Canadian Pacific Railway. Teenager Edward Mallandaine, known as "the Craigellachie Kid," can be seen peeking over Smith's shoulder, a lad among men. GLENBOW MUSEUM ARCHIVES

carefully tapped the new spike several times, not attempting the wallop that a trained rail worker would stroke. With an assured sense of timing, Edward Mallandaine leaned into the moment just as Ross took the second photograph. Smith tapped once more, and the steel vibrated loudly. The spike sank home.

The fading mountain echo of hammer on steel went still. No one breathed. Then a yelp broke loose, in what one writer claims to have been the voice of an excited child. Before Edward Mallandaine was done his yelp, hundreds of voices were whooping with him, sharing the confident knowledge that the dream of a truly national Canada, joined east to west, was coming true.

The crowd encouraged Van Horne to make a speech. His speech was rather terse, at a mere fifteen words long: "All I can say is that the work has been well done in every way."

Mallandaine had watched Donald Smith's first attempt, saw the bent spike yanked out and tossed onto the railbed, from where Van Horne's secretary, Arthur Piers, nonchalantly pocketed it (only to be called out later by Smith, who asked for it). Smith later had the "historic" spike split into lengthwise slivers, each affixed with a diamond, and then gave them to various women who were close to one of the company's executives.

As he was shouldered aside by the bigger men around him, Mallandaine had had to strain to keep his spot when photographer Ross again prepared his camera. When Smith's second "last spike" was successfully driven home, however, it would not remain in place for long. Roadmaster Frank Brothers foresaw a treasure hunters' rush if it was left in place, and chose to avoid the resulting havoc. As guests and audience moved away, Brothers removed the spike and later presented it to Edward Beatty, who became president of the CPR in 1918.

What Mallandaine and everyone else there could not have known at the time was that this same morning, 160 kilometres (107 miles) east of Eagle Pass at a place near Donald, thirty CPR workers, along with two North-West Mounted Police officers, waited on the main-line track for an eastbound transport. Realizing their delay was because of the event down-rail at Craigellachie, they mocked up their own ceremony and drove their own version of "The Last Spike."

Tales would soon swirl regarding a fourth "Last Spike," one not driven that day, although it was intended to be. The governor-general of Canada, the Marquis of Lansdowne, had planned to participate in the ceremony at Eagle Pass and had a silver spike made for his use. Van Horne heard of this and dismissed it. He held a view that the occasion should be less auspicious. Aware of the Union Pacific's carnival approach in 1869 at Promontory, Utah, with its gold spike, band, and festivities, Van Horne declared that the CPR's last spike would be iron—no gold or silver, these being frequent markers for railroads that later went bust. As matters turned out, Lansdowne was occupied elsewhere and his rejected silver spike was subsequently presented by the Governor-General to William Van Horne.

As young Edward Mallandaine watched the first two "last spikes" being driven, the world he lived in was rapidly changing. The new railroad opened a direct trade route from Europe to Atlantic Canada and across Canada to Port Moody, from where Canadian Pacific Steamships would access the wealth of Asia. Port Moody would turn out to be a temporary terminus for that route; Van Horne later told Port Moody officials, despite their protests, that he planned to run a spur line twenty-five kilometres (sixteen miles) farther west. Then the *Montreal Star* printed an article that announced, "The name of Vancouver has been chosen by Mr. Van Horne for the terminus at Coal Harbour, on Burrard Inlet."

Edward Mallandaine played a significant role in helping to grow the thriving country he witnessed coming together. He helped build British Columbia as an architect and surveyor, and co-founded the town of Creston, where he lived well for many years. He died in 1949 at the age of eighty-two, by which time the CPR's transcontinental railway was firmly established as the lifeline of the country.

PROMISES, PROMISES

THE FUTURE WAS FILLED with promise when the Colony of Vancouver Island was founded in 1849. Across the Strait of Georgia, and adding to the region's aspirations, came the 1858 establishment of the Colony of British Columbia. In 1866, the two outposts aligned politically, and New Westminster on the mainland relinquished its role as capital to Victoria on Vancouver Island, a status made final when British Columbia joined the Dominion of Canada as a province in 1871. In view of the city's increased stature, the federal government promised that Victoria would become the western terminus of Canada's national railway network.

John A. Macdonald had been knighted for his role in nation building on July 1, 1867, as the new country came into being with him as its first prime minister. Along with the designation "Sir," Macdonald could have as easily been labelled "the railway promiser." His later, much-trumpeted commitment to build a rail link from central Canada across the prairies to BC had eventually clinched the deal for BC's entry into the Dominion.

In fact, a defter "promiser of trains" was George-Étienne Cartier, Macdonald's minister of militia and defence. During Macdonald's first term of office, he was frequently sidetracked by illness. When that happened, Cartier acted as Macdonald's stand-in. It was on such an occasion, in spring 1870, that a delegation from BC, comprised of Victoria's Dr. John Helmcken and the Honorable Joseph W. Trutch, and Dr. Robert William Carrall from the Cariboo, visited Ottawa seeking a wagon road to the West. It was Cartier who upped

·the ante to a railroad. Cartier subsequently took the lead in negotiations of the BC–Canada terms of union, and it was his initiative that led to the creation of the CPR, creating the groundwork for Victoria's destiny as the orphan of the transcontinental railway family.

Macdonald was an adamant supporter of BC entering Confederation and the building of the railroad. Less so was Parliament, but it eventually supported the terms of union. Flowing from this was the prime minister's further promise that Victoria would be the final western stop of tracks on Canada's national railway.

When the union was finalized in 1871, the Dominion absorbed much of the new province's existing debt, and BC's voters were optimistic about the arrangements. The Dominion's viability, or lack of it, hinged on a railway being built within ten years of the celebrations. "Bonds of steel as well as of sentiment were needed to hold the new Confederation together," wrote George Stanley in his book *The Canadians*. But the post-Confederation calendar flipped toward 1881 all too quickly for the politicians and railroad builders.

The initial plan was to directly link Montreal by rail all the way to Vancouver Island. The plan called for tracks to be laid to Bute Inlet, over 200 kilometres (120 miles) up the mainland coast from Vancouver. From where the tracks ended on the mainland, a bridge would be built to carry them to Sonora Island and then Quadra Island and on to Vancouver Island. The rail line would continue to Victoria, the promised terminus.

In spring 1873, the federal government adopted this flawed plan bred of politics that wanted to secure new borders for a growing country at all costs. The proposition lacked the practical base of in-depth surveying and engineering studies. Contrarians felt a southern route to Port Moody would more affordably meet the obligations of a transcontinental railroad. From Port Moody, freight barges could service Vancouver Island.

Victoria was not amused.

In 1873, Macdonald took steps to address this discontent with a compromise. He now promised that the shipping and naval port of Esquimalt near Victoria would become the southern terminus of a railway between there and resource-rich Nanaimo, 110 kilometres (65 miles) up-Island, the home of large coal deposits. The House of Commons passed an Act of Parliament that would have given birth to the Esquimalt–Nanaimo Railway, but the Senate rejected it in 1875.

Victoria was not alone in its frustrations. The country's rail promises seemed in disarray and perhaps undeliverable. The government finally contracted a syndicate for the transcontinental railway's construction in 1880. Clearly, the prime minister's pledge to connect "the seaboard of BC with the railway system of Canada" within ten years had not come about.

British Columbia's government, unhappy with the delays in beginning railroad construction on Vancouver Island, threatened to withdraw from the legal deal that had brought them into Confederation, knowing the border to the south would prove flexible if BC wanted to join the US. Understandably, the US cast a covetous eye toward the colony-turned-province. The US had recently acquired Alaska from Russia in the summer of 1867 (for $7.2 million). Annexing BC to their jurisdiction would provide continuous land between the continental US and their new northern territory.

BC's threat of separation was a viable alternative. Although completing the transcontinental railway and appeasing Vancouver Island were both part of what Macdonald called "a solemn bargain made between Canada and British Columbia," securing BC and its Pacific Ocean access as part of Canada was Macdonald's truer aim.

The flamboyant Amor De Cosmos, a Victoria-based publisher and pro-Confederation activist, argued for the Esquimalt and Nanaimo Railway as a Member of Parliament. In May 1880, De Cosmos stood and delivered a passionate speech in Parliament, demanding that Ottawa make good on "its general expression of intention to keep faith with British Columbia." In answer to excuses of cost concerns, he admonished that "the expenditure will fall so lightly on the country" and pushed for the completion of the "continental portion" to Burrard Inlet, from where goods would use a "ferry to Nanaimo" and then freight and passengers would complete Canada's railway promise on the "Island Section of the Pacific Railway."

As was typical in North American rail construction, land grants, access points, and development privileges were perhaps even more important than the rights of trackage. Private interests, such as those of Nanaimo coal-mine baron Robert Dunsmuir, competed with the government-influenced (but cash-short) CPR. The winner would be enriched: the eventual land grants would approach 10 per-cent of Vancouver Island's 32,000 square kilometres (over 12,000 square miles).

Dunsmuir's proposal prevailed, and his Esquimalt and Nanaimo Railway Company came into being in summer 1886. The prime minister was invited to visit Victoria, but Macdonald had a pecu-liar relationship with the recalcitrant city. When his Conservative Party won the election of 1878, Macdonald lost his own seat due to the Pacific Scandal, in which he was seen to have taken funds in return for granting a railway contract. Although he was enthusiasti-cally acclaimed as a Member of Parliament for the Victoria electoral district, allowing him to sit in Parliament, he never visited the place as its representative.

Prime Minister Macdonald made his only sojourn to BC, and his former riding of Victoria, in 1886. He disembarked from his special train in Port Moody on July 9, four days after CPR's inau-gural passenger train had arrived at the terminus. From there he travelled to Shawnigan Lake on Vancouver Island, forty kilome-tres (twenty-five miles) north of Victoria, where he swung a silver

The E&N has been called a "consolation prize" from a government whose railway promisors failed to deliver. E&N DIVISION, CANADIAN RAIL-ROAD HISTORICAL ASSOCIATION

hammer to drive home a railway-completing gold spike at Cliffside. The E&N was a railroad, though Victoria was not yet serviced. Expansion of the rail line followed in 1887 and 1888, the year tracks finally reached Victoria.

Though controversy would not let go of Dunsmuir and the syndicate he headed (of which he owned 50 percent) the railway did not suffer. Fish, lumber (finished or raw for export), fruits, vegetables, and cattle—separated, of course, from the travelling public—all moved to market as the E&N prospered. Its reputation as a steam railway, home to workers with pride, grew. Even so, the E&N has been called a "consolation prize" from a government whose railway promisers failed to deliver.

In 1905, the CPR would get its hands on the E&N with a $1 million purchase from James Dunsmuir, the coal baron's son and a former premier of BC. That payment was for the railway alone; the lands not sold or leased by the Dunsmuirs were purchased separately. CPR extended the E&N northward to Comox and westward to Port Alberni, in total exceeding 200 kilometres (120 miles) of rail on Vancouver Island.

The E&N's service on Vancouver Island since its construction eventually became a hallmark of inconsistency, with passenger service interrupted for many years at a time and currently suspended, though the rails are used for limited freight traffic. The ownership has varied over the years, and the changes in responsibility for maintenance and scheduling have contributed to a reputation of unpredictability, including name changes—though to Islanders, it has always been known as the "E&N," even when that was not its official name. Rumours often bolster hope, more so than unfulfilled government promises, despite the former suggesting at the time of this book's publication that the E&N passenger train will soon be refashioned into service for travellers. Could it be, after nearly a century and a half since BC joined Confederation, that Macdonald's promise to link the country by rail might permanently come true?

AS SMOOTH AS SILK

THE CHILDREN WOULD WATCH with rapt attention as the flurry of activity unfolded before their eyes. Moments after the ship docked in Vancouver, the first bales of the precious cargo were unloaded by longshoremen. With practised precision, the bales were moved swiftly from ship to shore to boxcar. The assembled consist (a group of cars or coaches and engine that form a train) of waiting cars filled rapidly, and as the last bale was loaded in each car, it was sealed, not to be touched again until the train was unloaded with similar speed in New York. Then, with the release of high-pressure steam from whistles and pistons, another silk train would leave the waterfront with ever-increasing momentum.

Silk trains: the name itself sounds smooth and fast, and they were. High-speed trains are emblems of our own millennium but have been around for a long time. Fast trains of earlier generations once rushed silk across the continent, taking priority over all other forms of traffic. They operated from the late 1800s into the 1930s.

The rush of raw silk from the port of Vancouver to New York's National Silk Exchange thrilled all who watched the trains fly by at points along the way. Their speed was driven by the value and fragility of the product. Raw silk carried an enormous price at the time, with bales measuring almost a metre per side often valued at more than $800. An entire trainload might have approached $6 million in value a century ago, and armed guards would be on-board to protect the pricey cargo.

The reason for the rush was simple: the silk is made from the cocoons of silkworms, and thousands of cocoons are required to make even a small item of clothing. The perishable cargo and short life cycle of the silkworm made timing crucial at every step of the way. From the moment the eggs were laid through the month-long growth process, the race was on to deliver the finished product to the east coast.

The silk that arrived in Vancouver from Asia was offloaded onto specially designed railcars in less than two hours. With the fear of the cargo's deterioration foremost in shippers' minds, the perishable product was transported in airtight boxcars with interiors lined in varnished wood to help preserve the silk. Fifteen or more cars comprised a typical consist. When each car had been loaded with about 470 bales, sometimes in as few as eight minutes, and with a high-speed locomotive pulling the consist, the trains departed Vancouver and highballed it for the East. In some cases, the entire process from loading a ship in Japan to unloading the bales in New York could be accomplished in less than two weeks.

One can imagine how thrilled schoolchildren were to see this spectacle unfold, as they routinely did. Teachers would bring them dockside to watch the hurried process. Barked orders, rushing longshoremen hauling the cargo off the ships and into the railcars, and then that shriek from the locomotive whistle and that whoosh of steam cutting through the dockside air; it was an unforgettable sight for eyes young and old.

All other traffic took to sidings or sat waiting to be moved onto the main line until a silk train had passed. Passengers, freight, and at one point, the royal train carrying King George VI and his wife, Queen Elizabeth, on their 1939 Canadian tour, all waited for the speeding silker to rush down the rails.

Crews and engines were changed frequently along the journey, with fresh locomotives ready and waiting as the train approached the end point in each division. Locomotive change times of less than ten minutes were typical, and with a new engine and crew, and quick maintenance and lubrication done, the train tore on. The speed alone, often over a hundred kilometres (sixty-two miles) an hour, caught the attention of all who saw one pass. A typical cross-country trip would take many hours less than even the fastest express passenger train. One report told of a silk train making the crossing in three days, beating a typical passenger consist by over thirty hours, though this claim is thought dubious by some.

The CPR and CNR competed with each other to deliver the silk to east-coast markets. The lightweight cars used by both railroads were designed to shorter lengths than were typical and were mounted on passenger-train trucks (sprung-wheel assemblies), which made for a smoother ride.

Things changed when the stock market tumbled in 1929 and the demand for luxury products like silk crashed along with it. With the high revenues previously enjoyed by the railroads slipping dramatically, transporting silk by ship through the Panama Canal became a viable alternative. By the early 1930s, the number of silk bales shipped by rail was plummeting, some of it travelling with regular passenger consists. The advent of war with Japan in 1941 put the silk trade to seemingly final rest. By the time the market could recover after the war, the product had been replaced in large part by synthetics.

The specially designed silk-train cars were repurposed to regular baggage cars and assigned other uses. The last of the lot ended its working life in ignominious fashion as a weed-control car, which sprayed the tracks and gravel ballast supporting them with herbicide.

The silkers weren't the only high-speed trains in the early years of the twentieth century. Almost a hundred years ago, the Fraser Valley city of Mission adopted the moniker "Strawberry Capital of the World," as verdant truck farms on its North Fraser River location produced bumper crops of the bright-red berries. Mission thrived with two resources in those days, strawberries and cedar shakes. BC's

Lower Mainland absorbed much of the strawberry crop, but there was plenty left over that could be delivered to markets both east and south, and so it was that priority trains left Mission to take this perishable crop away at high speed in refrigerated cars.

The war intervened in 1941, and local truck farming of strawberries declined due to a variety of economic and social reasons, including competition from cheaper products from the US and the internment of many Japanese truck farmers. Mission never regained its dominance in this market, but memories remain of the high-speed trains that rushed their tasty treats east and south.

The highballed runs of the fast trains weren't always smooth. In September 1927, just a few kilometres from Yale, up the Fraser River from Vancouver, ten cars of a silk train's consist flew off the rails. Some $1.5 million in raw silk ended up in the Fraser River. Locals called it "the million-dollar wreck." Some bales were recovered by local residents, but their value had plummeted because of their immersion in the water. There are unconfirmed rumours of another loss farther west in the valley a couple of years later. In that case, reports say the recovered cargo was loaded onto regular freight cars for the remainder of the journey.

Today's network of interprovincial and interstate highways provides efficient delivery of produce to all locations in North America. International delivery of perishables can be accomplished by an overnight flight. The day of the silk trains is long gone, but the rush of a high-speed train passing through town, carrying precious cargo to far-off markets, lingers in some memories still.

POETRY IN LOCOMOTION
Yukon's Bard Arrives by Train

There's a land where the mountains are nameless,
And the rivers all run God knows where...
ROBERT SERVICE, "The Spell of the Yukon"

THIRTY-YEAR-OLD Robert William Service, with a Victorian bank teller's demeanor and suited attire, sat aboard the slow-moving White Pass and Yukon Route Railroad as its steam engine struggled against the track's incline and the train fought its way up the mountain from Skagway, Alaska, toward Yukon. The coaches carried an assortment of fortune seekers, each filled with uncertainty about their prospects, as was Service. Winds buffeted the consist as autumn gave way to winter in one of the world's harshest environments.

It was early November 1904, and the Canadian Bank of Commerce had transferred the English-born Service from its branch in Kamloops. His new posting awaited him nearly 160 kilometres (100 miles) up the track from Skagway, in Whitehorse, a town that eight years earlier was a traditional First Nations hunting and fishing location that was quickly becoming a prospectors' camp, without a single building, let alone a bank. Now, the town bustled with frontier enthusiasms as mining, industry, and newcomers took root, settling in for the long term. The blazing gold fever was over, but not the entrepreneurial spirit. Most of the stampeders of the Klondike Gold Rush of 1898 had left. Much of Yukon's lustrous allure had gone with them, and Robert Service was just the man to polish it up again, this time with words instead of gold.

Service wrote in his autobiography, *Ploughman of the Moon: An Adventure into Memory*, that "Skagway was wreathed in rain when I took the train for White Horse. But immediately the snow began and soon there were six feet of it on either side of the climbing track. Far below I could see the old trail of ninety-eight."

The WP&YR rolling stock hugged the rock wall on the inside of what a traveller described as "the nearly perpendicular slopes of the White Pass," where engineers had carved a rail route against all known logic of railroad building. (The pass was named after Sir Thomas White, then Canada's minister of the interior.) The railbed beneath had been blasted into being with 450 tons of explosives, the Mile 16 tunnel drilled and sculpted by tenacious but often unwilling workers during the 1888 winter that took temperatures down to −60°F (−51°C). History had given the railroad its moniker "Railway Built of Gold," but the construction workers knew it by a truer name, "The Railroad to Hell."

On Service's journey, the train curled tight into a sixteen-degree turn. Building that turn had been an engineering feat made even more challenging by a grade approaching 3.9 percent. All construction of the three-metre-wide (ten-foot) roadbed had been risky, of both lives and investment. The hazards for workers were harrowing. Cost risks were intimidating, too, only partially ameliorated by use of a narrow-gauge track nine-tenths of a metre (three feet) wide, a design decision that allowed for a sharper radius on curves and a more manageable financial gamble.

Service acknowledged the benefits that resulted: "Had not my ticket, for about a hundred miles of transportation, cost me twenty-five dollars?"

Service was riding on a railway birthed by a gold rush the likes of which the world had never seen. In summer 1897, one headline on the front page of the *Seattle Post-Intelligencer* had blared, "Gold! Gold! Gold!" The steamship *Portland* had arrived in Seattle the day before, greeted by five thousand people. Aboard were sixty-eight miners and their bags of Yukon gold—rich men with stories of finding motherlodes and creeks offering nuggets for the picking. Greed, craving, and the promise of adventure hung in the air.

In summer 1896, Skookum Jim (Keish was his Native name) and Dawson Charlie (Ḵáa Goox), along with California-born prospector George Carmack, had discovered gold in Yukon. They'd first panned shiny specks in the waters of Rabbit Creek. According to Carmack, they "turned over loose pieces of rock and found gold that lay thick between the flaky slabs like cheese sandwiches." Within twenty-four hours, Skookum Jim, Dawson Charlie, and George Carmack had staked their claims and renamed the location Bonanza Creek. The Klondike Gold Rush was on.

At that time, Robert Service had not yet met the adventurers who would prompt him to write,

> You who this faint day the High North is luring
> Unto her vastness, taintlessly sweet;
> You who are steel-braced, straight-lipped, enduring,
> Dreadless in danger and dire in defeat...
> "Men of the High North"

When gold seekers arrived in Skagway to make their way north to the goldfields, they had two route options. The most popular was the rugged Chilkoot Pass, a trail of the Tlingit people, the name a derivative of their word *Tschilkut*. The trail was fifty-three kilometres (thirty-three miles) long, beginning in Dyea, near Skagway, and leading to Lake Bennett in Canada. The prospectors climbed to 1,067 metres (3,502 feet) above sea level. The formidable step-by-step trek became notorious as "The Golden Stairs."

Another trail, leading away from the Alaska tidewaters to Lake Bennett had recently been surveyed, and the climbers found it to be less steep than the Chilkoot, though just as rough and demanding. Its summit was reached at 879 metres (2,885 feet) after 32 kilometres (20 miles) of hard travel out of Skagway.

The Chilkoot Trail and the White Pass Trail merged at the southern end of Lake Bennett. Here the prospectors had to hand-saw lumber to make their boats for the long journey down Lake Bennett, past Caribou Crossing, through Miles Canyon and Whitehorse Rapids, and then to Whitehorse, by which time they were 177 kilometres (110 miles) from Skagway. From Whitehorse, the hardy continued in their boats on the Yukon River, navigating the Whitehorse Rapids on their way to Dawson City. There, for the lucky few, gold awaited. But first for many, a new law would command their attention.

Prospectors climbing either the Chilkoot or White Pass crossed from the US into Canada; the international borderline on the pass's trailheads was then poorly defined. Colonel Samuel Benfield Steele of the North-West Mounted Police arrived to establish order. His customs posts quickly became sites of authority. Among his early actions were the creation and enforcement of a regulation stipulating that anyone wishing to cross into Canada must have with them "one ton" of supplies—the amount Steele reckoned they would need to support their quest and not become a burden.

Steele's decision created the need for gold seekers to make multiple trips up and down the mountain, a gruelling ritual that angered ill-prepared stampeders who anxiously wanted to get to the gold-fields. Steele was firm. American authorities questioned his right to rule but deferred because, as one Canadian put it, "It was a case of possession being ten points in the law, and we intend to hold possession." Steele ruled over the only two access routes to the Klondike, the summit of each pass eventually being included within Canada with the 1899 establishment of an international boundary.

With thousands of future adventurers expected, officials of both countries feared unmanageable crowds. When the dangers of both the White Pass and the Chilkoot were added to the demands of stamina for the adventurers, plus the time and resources needed to make it to the Yukon, the need to build a railroad became paramount.

Robert Service would later listen to the stories of these Yukon adventurers and write of them,

> There's a race of men that don't fit in,
> A race that can't stay still;
> So they break the hearts of kith and kin,
> And they roam the world at will . . .
> "The Men That Don't Fit In"

In 1897, thirty-two business proposals for Yukon railroads were presented to the Canadian government, which anticipated a line from Skagway through Whitehorse to Fort Selkirk. The route and company selected to go from Skagway would require the collaboration of two nations, many partners, and several egos. But compared with rock cutting, and anchoring the roadbed to a mountainside, that could have been the easy part. However, nothing about this railroad would prove to be practicable. Serendipity played a role when Canadian railway contractor Michael Heney introduced himself to Sir Thomas Tancred in a Skagway saloon in 1898 after overhearing a conversation about the difficulty in constructing a railway over the White Pass route. Tancred brought an engineering background to their partnership and helpfully also had a relationship with Close Brothers of London, a firm of English investors who would eventually head a syndicate that boosted the dreams of a White Pass & Yukon Route Railroad into viability.

Tancred was also business pals with surveyor John Hislop, who was assisting the wispy, moustached Erastus Corning Hawkins. Hawkins was working on a feasibility study regarding a possible railroad, and had at the time erroneously concluded it was impossible to build. Heney changed his mind. Their new consortia would be joined by the pipe-smoking, bow-tied Samuel Graves, the railway's eventual president.

For the complex railroad project to succeed, it needed cooperative leadership as well ballasted as any railbed they would build. The men opted to align their ambitions with those of George Brackett, who was well along in building a wagon road to the White Pass: together, they attracted an investment of $10 million. Financing came mostly from the group in Britain. However, it was still vital to pursue land grants, secure labour, and outsmart the competition of proposed tramlines. Most of all, they needed to focus on priority number one: laying tracks to the White Pass Summit to transport miners and their provisions and deliver a financial return to willing but nervous investors.

The obstacles to building a railway up the White Pass route seemed insurmountable, the task treacherous. "Nearly every mile of roadbed had to be blasted with dynamite, and local timber proved useless for ties, bridges, and stringers," wrote Melody Webb in her book *Yukon: The Last Frontier.*

An engineering marvel, the 256-metre (840-foot) cantilevered bridge over a difficult gully along the Pass was often shrouded in low cloud. Recognized at the time as the tallest structure of its kind, it was exhilarating in its height and length. The dangers of this railroad's construction exploits stood out among railways around the world.

Robert Service and his fellow passengers that day in 1904 must have shared a feeling of relief when the train reached level ground

The first passenger train of the White Pass & Yukon Route Railway en route to a summit in Alaska, February 20, 1899. The WP&YR has been recognized as an International Historic Civil Engineering Landmark, a rare accolade, one also accorded to the Eiffel Tower and the Panama Canal. UNIVERSITY OF WASHINGTON LIBRARIES, SPECIAL COLLECTIONS, HEGG 661. PHOTOGRAPH BY ERIC A. HEGG

and a valley setting, eventually coming to a stop at Carcross (formerly Caribou Crossing), where the railway line's last spike had been driven. In the first year of the twentieth century, tracks built over difficult terrain northward from Lake Bennett had finally met tracks lain south from Whitehorse, enabling the trains like the one Service rode to travel all the way from Skagway to Whitehorse.

When Robert Service was in Carcross, the story of WP&YR president Samuel Graves's, escapade while driving the last spike would have still been making the rounds. As Graves recounted it, on July 29, 1900, the first spike to be driven had proved too soft for the job, even though it was gold and beautiful. Graves asked an American colonel to give "the last spike the first blow." The colonel had missed "by several inches." Another gentleman stepped forward and "gave the spike a lady-like tap on the head and looked like he was laying carpets." The next man "had partaken of much refreshment until he had overdone the process and could see two spikes." His smack left "a pretty tired spike when it came to my turn to drive it home," wrote Graves. "I didn't hit it quite fair, and the spike was bent as before. In the middle of this, the corner of my eye caught the foreman sneaking up with a spike puller which he stealthily applied to the dilapidated last spike."

An iron spike was inserted, driven home, and the railway was declared finished. The once-impossible project had been completed in twenty-six months with the help of nearly 35,000 workers. The next year frequently saw peak rail traffic of four trains a day.

Leaving behind Carcross and heading farther north, the cold and dark and unfamiliar landscape would not have been lost on Service as his train took him ever closer to his new life and the anecdotes he would listen to and write about:

> There are strange things done in the midnight sun
> By the men who moil for gold;
> The Arctic trails have their secret tales
> That would make your blood run cold...
> "The Cremation of Sam McGee"

At the head of Robert Service's train was likely a steam engine built by Grant Locomotive Works, a 2-8-0 built in 1882 and retired in 1907. It was a bit of a lush when it came to fuel and said to be "a guzzler" of water on the steep incline, a reputation that labelled such engines as "hogs," and by extension, their drivers as "hogheads."

Service arrived at the Whitehorse depot at the centre of town, the surveyors for WP&YR having set the railway's terminus at the intersection of Front and Main Streets. At the station, Service stepped off the train and into a future as a writer of remarkable poetry that would resonate for generations.

The first extended long poem Service published was "The Shooting of Dan McGrew," in 1906, followed by "The Cremation of Sam McGee." Over the years, others, such as "The Spell of the Yukon," would follow.

In 1908, the bank transferred Service to Dawson City, then the capital of Yukon. There he retired to full-time writing in 1909, keeping a residence in Dawson for three more years.

When Service wrote these lines in "The Parson's Son," he might have thought such words also true about the White Pass and Yukon Route Railway:

I'm one of the Arctic brotherhood, I'm an old-time pioneer.
I came with the first—O God! how I've cursed this Yukon—
but I'm still here...

In 1912, Robert Service boarded the WP&YR for a final southbound journey. He was never to return, though he would forever be known as "The Bard of the Yukon."

DESPERATION
AND DISASTERS

THINGS CAN GO as horribly wrong with a train, as they can with any mode of transportation. Human error, ill intent, unforeseen circumstances, and a desperate need for coal in the depths of a Canadian winter are some of the factors involved in these tales of rail trips gone wrong.

◀ The West Coast Railway Heritage Park near Squamish, British Columbia, offers a day-long adventure exploring the 2860 Royal Hudson Locomotive, heritage rail cars, and numerous other locomotives, displays, and reconstructed buildings. **PHOTO BY DAVID THOMSON**

"THIS IS A HOLDUP.
GIVE US YOUR COAL!"

DAY AND NIGHT, trains laden with coal criss-cross the North American continent. Giant machines helmed by hard-rock miners who grind away at coal faces, above ground or deep beneath it, empty the rich basins that bear this compressed carbon and load it into purpose-built rail cars for transport.

Much of today's black bounty heads offshore to power China, by far the world's largest user of coal-fired power-generating plants. Some is destined for the American heartland. Six Canadian provinces use coal in generating power. But few today remember the role that coal played in heating North American homes just a few decades ago, before oil, gas, and then electric heat became the most common sources of central heating.

The town of Nanton, Alberta, remembers. In the winter of 1907, Nanton was running out of coal to burn in the fireplaces and furnaces that protected the town's residents from the harsh, bitter cold of the prairie winter. Coal, such a common mineral, became worth its weight in its lustrous cousin as supplies dried up. In 1906, a strike paralyzed much of Canada's coal-mining industry, and supplies began to run low across the country. With temperatures dipping to forty below, Nanton's lack of access to coal was becoming desperate.

With temperatures that cold, exposed flesh can freeze in seconds. Settlers on the Canadian Prairies had decades of experience dealing with winter's coldest blows, and Nanton residents knew their

This postcard published by Rumsey & Company, Toronto, shows Nanton, Alberta, circa 1907.

survival depended on keeping warm. But the coal trains that passed town in February 1907 didn't stop. American suppliers were still able to send their commodity north via the Canadian Pacific Railway (CPR), but other communities had purchased those shipments, and volumes were still far below what was needed. Nanton was not scheduled to be on the delivery list for some time yet.

Nanton lies a little more than eighty kilometres (fifty miles) south of Calgary, the oil capital of Canada. A brightly coloured grain elevator stands today at the side of the abandoned track bed. The land around is essentially flat, like much of Southern Alberta, with the occasional hillock rising in a low profile that briefly obscures the horizon. Just over 2,100 people call Nanton home these days, but a century ago, the town's population would have numbered only a few hundred. This is farming country, and in those days, the familiar checkerboard of the Canadian prairies was just beginning to take shape. But in the depth of the 1907 winter, the checkerboard was covered in frozen snow, and the people of Nanton were suffering from the cold with no relief in sight.

Day after day, the townsfolk watched CPR trains from the south carrying coal for other destinations trundle through town without stopping, no doubt thinking their money was as good as any other town's, so why wouldn't the trains stop and give them the coal they needed? Finally, one train did make a short stop in Nanton, and a daring member of the town's suffering population made his move.

Ira Shoop boarded the train as it was starting to leave. He made his way forward, reportedly running atop the cars to the engine, where he pushed the engineer aside and set the brakes. No doubt the engineer tried to interrupt his brazen move, but Shoop would not be deterred and brought the train to a halt. Then townsfolk appeared at the side of the tracks, prepared to relieve the boxcars of their precious cargo, which they did, loading coal sacks and horse-drawn wagons and sleighs with coal. More came along, bringing more sacks and wagons, and joined the group liberating the coal from the idled cars.

Remarkably, no violence occurred, though local Mounted Police officer Constable Currie drew his weapon and fired a warning shot that townsfolk ignored. Currie and a few others pleaded with the throngs to stop, but to no avail. Nor could the train crew do anything to prevent the citizens from taking direct action, and after their initial pleas and objections, they simply stood by and watched as three boxcars were emptied of their prized cache of coal. It all proceeded with an eerie calm: Nanton's people felt their actions were justified, and they emptied the cars with a sense of duty to families and the community. If they did not act now, when might a shipment destined for Nanton arrive? And who would be left alive to unload the train? With diligence and dispatch, they took what they needed.

Still, Nanton was a town of good character, and this was no ordinary train robbery. The citizens handled the process properly, and distributed the coal quietly and efficiently. No riots, no disorderly drunks, no thievery in the night; all was done in the light of day, and when they were finished taking what they needed, the principled people of Nanton paid for it.

The going price for coal in 1907 was some six dollars a ton, and that was the price they paid. CPR officials could only take the money, recognizing, no doubt, that the citizens of Nanton had every right to live, and while they were willing to steal in order to do so, they also were willing to pay a fair price for their black booty. Reports don't say which towns were disadvantaged by the theft, but the populace in Nanton lived to thrive.

A BUCKLING TRAGEDY AT POINT ELLICE

BRITISH COLONIST, MAY 27, 1896, p. 1:

QUEEN VICTORIA'S birthday carnival, so auspiciously inaugurated with unalloyed enjoyment for citizens and visitors, was abruptly terminated yesterday afternoon by a catastrophe so sudden, so awful and so appalling in the loss of life entailed by it that no thought was left for aught besides.

ON THE AFTERNOON of May 26, 1896, in Victoria, BC's capital city, events were in full swing to celebrate Queen Victoria's birthday.

At one p.m., a military band left the drill hall and marched along Government Street toward two ferry steamers waiting at the wharf at the end of Johnson Street. They were on their way to festivities at Point Macaulay (near Esquimalt) to inaugurate new forts. They had just landed at the barracks when whistles and bells sounded at a distance—generally a call for those designated to help suppress fire. The soldiers and sailors carried on together in a colourful sham fight and naval review, including a "march past" and three cheers for Queen Victoria—staged in front of the Lieutenant-Governor of BC. Little did they know what disaster was unfolding only a few kilometres away.

A streetcar is pulled from the harbour after the Point Ellice Bridge disaster in 1896. IMAGE A-02738, ROYAL BC MUSEUM AND ARCHIVES

Local residents and visitors were also heading for the military celebrations by railcar. Spectators would not likely see festivities from the water, so that very morning the *Colonist* had recommended that its readers "take the cars." Car 16 of the newly formed Consolidated Electric Railway Company was crammed and dangerously overloaded as it started to make its way across the Point Ellice Bridge just before two p.m.

The bridge had been built for the government in 1885 by the San Francisco Bridge Company, and was turned over to the city in 1891. In 1892, a rotten timber had snapped as a train made the crossing—fortunately, without incident—but the *Colonist* reported that the cause was identified as water working its way into bolt holes. Now, four years later, the bridge had weakened even more. Suddenly, the centre span buckled, and Car. 16 twisted and plummeted into the Gorge Waterway.

The *Colonist* reported that "the crashing timbers and ironwork of the bridge piled upon the ill-fated car as the waters received it, and, doubling up, pierced it also from below, so that many were killed even before the water was reached, while the others were less mercifully held below the muddy waters." Within an hour, thousands of people gathered at the harbour's edge with offers of help or to wait in agony for news of friends and family. Sadly, fifty-five men, women, and children had lost their lives, and the entire city shut down in shock and grief.

Even after nearly 120 years, it's one of the worst railway accidents in Western Canada.

On May 28, the *Colonist* wrote that William Gore, deputy commissioner of lands and works in BC had received a private telegram from San Francisco saying that in 1891, President McMullen of the San Francisco Bridge Company had warned him that the bridge was unsafe.

Gore, however, said he had no recollection of McMullen ever telling him the bridge was unsafe. "He was the man who built it, and it is not likely that he would make such a remark," he said.

A coroner's jury found that the Consolidated Electric Railway Company was directly responsible for having allowed overloading, and that the City of Victoria was guilty of contributory negligence for lack of maintenance. Undaunted by the jury's findings and the company's bankruptcy, financial backers reorganized and less than a year later, incorporated the British Columbia Electric Railway Company in order to take over three street railways in BC. . . After the bridge collapse, a temporary bridge was built and then replaced by a permanent structure in 1904.

TERRORISM ON THE TRACKS

PEEK INTO BRITISH COLUMBIA'S rail history, and you'll find many intriguing whodunit mysteries to unravel. Many involve explosives and intent to destroy property and perhaps human life.

One such mystery—still unsolved—began to unfold just after 1:00 a.m. on October 29, 1924, one mile west of Farron, a tiny community southwest of Nelson in southeastern BC.

Conductor Joseph Turner was on duty aboard Train No. 11 when it left Nelson at 11:20 a.m. on October 28. The mail car, baggage car, first-class day coach, and sleeper car were headed east on the Kettle Valley Railway. At Brilliant, Peter Verigin and his companion (not his wife of many years), seventeen-year-old Marie Strelaeff, boarded the day coach. Conductor Turner recognized Verigin and punched out a cash fare to Grand Forks for the two passengers.

Sixty-five-year-old Verigin was well known in the area. As a religious leader of the Doukhobors, who had emigrated to Canada from Russia in 1902 for religious and political reasons, he had, in 1908, led about six thousand followers from Saskatchewan to southeastern BC in hopes of establishing a communal settlement.

Another well-known man aboard the train was forty-nine-year-old John McKie, who sat two seats ahead of Verigin on the same side. McKie, the Member of the Legislative Assembly (MLA) for Grand Forks–Greenwood, was on his way to the opening of the legislature in Victoria.

At 12:20 a.m., Train No. 11 pulled into Farron, where crews "cleaned the engine fire" (by breaking up clinkers—the stony residue from burned coal—and distributing burning coal evenly inside the firebox), took on water, and picked up the café car.

"Nothing unusual happened to attract my attention in any way at this point," Turner later recalled. "I got on the front end of the day coach leaving Farron, and walked through to the rear end. All the passengers were in either a dozing or sleeping attitude. Mr. Veregin [*sic*] had his head bent over as if in a dozing position. The lady, who was on the window side, was leaning toward the window and also in a dozing attitude."

A newspaper seller named Mr. Fawcett was asleep in a double seat at the forward end of the car, on the south side.

On reaching the rear of the train, Conductor Turner joined trainman Wilfred Marquis on the platform. Marquis was a new employee, and the two men chatted about steam heat; steam was working throughout the train. Then they walked through the sleeper and the day coach to the baggage car.

Less than a minute later, an explosion rocked the day coach. It was so powerful that it blew away the baggage-car end door, showering Turner and Marquis with broken glass from the day-coach windows. The train stopped almost immediately.

"We saw right through the end doorway of the baggage car at what was left of the day coach, and it was practically demolished. We observed fire in the body of the coach... it had a yellow tinge. We also observed a flame that was coming from somewhere under the coach on the outside, and on the same side, of a blue colour," said Turner.

Turner barked at the crew to find the fire extinguishers. He then turned his attention to the injured. "We tore away the broken pieces of the car at the west and liberated three: two men and a woman and assisted them into the baggage car. We then liberated three more at the east end."

By this time, the fire was gaining headway and burning toward the east end. Fumes of gas escaping from the tanks forced Turner and the crew to get out. No one seemed to be alive when they left.

Amid the chaos and groans, Turner organized the passengers and crew to help the injured to the sleeper; then he rushed back along the tracks to Farron.

In all, nine people died as a result of the explosion, including Verigin, Strelaeff, and McKie.

Within hours, word spread that the Doukhobor leader had died. Perhaps no train station ever saw such a display of grief as was reported in the *Nelson Daily News* the next day:

> A great wail of despair and grief went up from nearly a thousand Doukhobors, community and independent, on the platform at Brilliant, when the train from Nelson to Rossland pulled in yesterday at 2 o'clock p.m., and the crowds of Doukhobors aboard confirmed the news of Peter Verigin's death.

Police, CPR officials, explosive experts, and others rushed to the scene—which, interestingly, could only be accessed by rail. Rumours immediately began to circulate. What had caused the explosion? Had it been an accident or something more sinister?

Two inquests ensued: one convened the next night in Grand Forks, the second in Nelson a few days later.

Constable Edward House of the CPR and Staff-Sergeant Cammon of the Provincial Police at Nelson had examined the disaster scene at noon the same day. House reported to the Grand Forks inquest:

> About fifty feet [fifteen metres] up the hill on a bank we found a part of a dry cell battery and down where the car was burned, we found the remains of an alarm clock. I took possession of the

battery and clock. On examination there appears to be a piece of wire soldered to one of the cog-wheels. We only found one clock. I could form no definite conclusion as to the cause of the explosion except that a high explosive was used. My theory from finding the clock and the battery is that a time bomb was used. There would be no place in the equipment of the coach for such a battery as that found. The gas tanks and the steam pipes on the car were intact.

The coroner's jury agreed, and in their verdict urged the CPR and the provincial authorities to continue their efforts to find who was responsible for the disaster and to determine ownership of the battery and clock.

Who would have wanted to kill Verigin, and why? The Doukhobors were a divided community, and not all supported Verigin—for economic, personal, and religious reasons. Were there other BC residents who violently disagreed with his particular brand of Doukhobor philosophy? Might the plot have involved the Canadian or Russian governments?

McKie, a Conservative, could also have been the target. A BC provincial election earlier that year had resulted in Liberals winning twenty-four of the forty-eight seats. With the legislature set to open on November 3, a Liberal Speaker of the House had to be selected. With McKie out of the way, Premier Oliver could then enjoy a majority of one.

Today, a disaster of this magnitude would see investigators working long and hard to crack the case. But in 1924, police officers could only allocate one or two days. No one was ever charged, and the mystery remains unsolved.

Other random, mysterious terrorist acts occurred in southern BC in the 1950s and early 1960s. Media reports alleged that these were linked to a radical sect of the Doukhobors in the Kootenays who protested the Canadian government's perceived interference in their lives. Non-violent protests took the form of public nudity and refusing to pay taxes but could also include targeting the CPR, resulting in surveillance by the RCMP.

In October 1952, CPR tracks and a boxcar were heavily damaged when dynamite exploded under the car on a siding near Skaha Lake.

In other such incidents, the bombs at first consisted of a few sticks tied together with enough fuse to allow the criminals time to clear the track before the bombs exploded. Usually, only a few feet of track were destroyed, damage which could be detected by "speeder cars" inspecting the track in advance of trains. But in 1958, the RCMP became increasingly concerned when the terrorists began to mine the tracks with percussion caps that would potentially explode when a train ran over them.

In January 1958, a passenger train derailed when a bomb went off twenty-nine kilometres (eighteen miles) east of Grand Forks, damaging ninety-two metres (three hundred feet) of track. No passengers were hurt. That same month, sixteen sticks of dynamite with a fuse attached were discovered on CPR tracks one kilometre south of the West Summerland station. The track was part of the CPR's Kettle Valley line from Hope through Summerland to Penticton and on to Grand Forks and the Kootenays. There was enough explosive power to destroy a locomotive or vaporize anybody running over it on a speeder.

Some railway workers driving to and from work were stopped by police, who opened trunks to ensure the workers weren't smuggling dynamite.

At 2:40 a.m. on June 7, 1958, a powerful blast shook Princeton. The police couldn't locate the site of the explosion, but advised the Penticton train dispatcher to warn trains to be on the lookout for track damage.

A westbound freight train was due, and fortunately the dispatcher alerted the section foreman at Belfort to warn the train's crew as it passed while descending Jura Hill. The engineer crept down the rest of the hill and, fortunately, stopped the train in time when the damage from the blast suddenly appeared in front of them.

On July 28, 1958, more bombings occurred. This time, the Canadian National Railway was hit when a fifty-six centimetre (twenty-two-inch) section of track was demolished in an explosion forty-seven kilometres (twenty-nine miles) south of Vernon.

The other explosion was at Oliver, ninety-six kilometres (sixty miles) to the south; it ripped a small hole under CPR tracks, delaying the regular fruit train by one hour.

In his book *Lions in the Coquihalla,* former railroad yardmaster Arnold Palm recalled that in the Kootenays, large steel railway bridges were floodlit and protected by armed guards who manned machine-gun posts at each end of the bridges, twenty-four hours a day.

Even though a guard was on duty on December 11, 1961, terrorists using an estimated thirty sticks of dynamite blew up a huge chunk of a railway bridge twenty-four kilometres (fifteen miles) west of Nelson and ripped up a section of track near the community of Shoreacres.

These incidents and others in and around the Okanagan and Kootenays declined after 1962, when thirty-six Doukhobor sect members were convicted of arson or conspiracy to commit arson and sentenced to prison terms. Whether all, or indeed any, of the terrorist attacks on the tracks were Doukhober-related remains a mystery.

HARD LUCK LOCOMOTIVE NUMBER ONE

SEPTEMBER 1926. A westbound freight train on the Kettle Valley Railroad in the Coquihalla Pass stopped at the summit to pick up cars that had been left behind by another train. To the train's original consist, the crew added several more cars that were loaded with coal. They also had a pusher locomotive and caboose on the trailing end to help them reach the summit. These now would go downhill with them to Hope, where the crew would uncouple the pusher, which would then assist another train on the eastbound climb back up to the summit.

As they started the run down to Hope, the lead locomotive lost brake pressure. The pusher crew gaped in horror as the train gathered speed, now a downhill runaway. They saw the trainmen atop the cars, frantically trying to apply the handbrakes, but the runaway didn't slow. Desperate to uncouple themselves from the runaway, the fireman worked his way to the front of the engine and reached for the uncoupling lever. With an opened throttle pushing the runaway, the fireman had enough slack and was able to uncouple the pusher from the rest of the train. Then, as they followed it down the hill at a much slower speed, with their own brakes in dire straits, the head end left the rails and slammed into the canyon below.

The wreckage was on fire when crews arrived to help, too late. Several bodies, perhaps eight to ten, were found around the crash site, but there had been only four crew members on the train. Reports said that a number of men had been hovering near the train at the summit station, perhaps intending to sneak aboard once the train started rolling. Had they jumped or fallen off along the runaway route? Or did they not sneak aboard in the first place? No one knows for sure, but it appeared that all aboard the runaway perished.

Locomotive 3563 being re-railed in Vancouver's Glen Yard in 1956, just prior to being lost in the Fraser River. **PETER LAYLAND, COURTESY OF *THE VANCOUVER SUN***

HARD LUCK LOCOMOTIVE NUMBER TWO

LOCOMOTIVE NO. 3563 was a CN Mikado. A Mikado is a large steam locomotive with the wheel arrangement 2-8-2: two wheels on the leading truck, eight driving wheels, and two on the trailing truck. No. 3563 had suffered a derailment in Vancouver's Glen Yard and required extensive repair work. A picture of the derailment scene shows No. 3563 straddling three sets of tracks in the yard and tilted at a precarious angle. Repairs were made at the Glen Yard, and then the thirty-three-year-old locomotive was reassigned for service based at the Port Mann Yard, east of Vancouver, on the south bank of the Fraser River.

On November 6, 1956, engineer Mike Nikolaieff, fireman Bill Hicks and head-end brakeman Bev McCrae nursed No. 3563 out of the Port Mann Yard and headed for Boston Bar, up the Fraser Canyon. The tracks here follow the south shore of the Fraser River for miles, rolling past verdant farms and through small communities. East of Fort Langley, in the Glen Valley area, they slowed for a point on the line where some washouts had occurred. As a nighttime fog enveloped the locomotive, the crew neared a trestle, expecting to meet a watchman posted at the bridge. Because of previous close calls at this location, the watchman would walk ahead of the train to ensure safe passage. They moved forward slowly past a warning flag, then brought the engine to a sudden stop when they heard the watchman call out. Nikolaieff stepped down from the cab to discuss the situation with him. As they were considering moving ahead, the trestle suddenly collapsed with a loud noise and the locomotive and tender slid off the crumbling track and down into the water and mud below in seconds. McCrae and Hicks leapt away as the locomotive rolled onto its left side. They made it to safety just before the entire assemblage slid down the bank and into the Fraser River, six metres (twenty feet) below.

The *Vancouver Sun* report on November 8, 1956, quoted engineer Nikolaieff as saying, "There was no warning at all. She just hit a soft spot and rolled over."

The crew watched as the locomotive and tender disappeared into the river. Crews assessed the possibility of recovery, but that proved to be impossible. No. 3563 remains today where it sank that November night. Track extensions a few years later created a new roadbed over the accident site, and this hard-luck locomotive forms a solid steel foundation for the new rails above.

This story is recounted on former railroader Bruce Harvey's blog. For a more detailed version, and other railroad tales, see caboosecoffee.ca.

HARD LUCK LOCOMOTIVE NUMBER THREE

ON DECEMBER 15, 1967, a diesel locomotive, No. 9122, was leading a consist north through the Fraser Canyon, with three trainmen in the cab. As they entered one of the many tunnels on the route, they saw another locomotive, No. 9062, entering the other end of the tunnel at runaway speed, determined later to be sixty-seven kilometres (forty-two miles) per hour and heading straight for them. The engineer, Dave Lawson, started braking action while the other two men in the cab took cover low down. The collision of the locomotives was unavoidable, and before the engineer himself could take cover, the collapsing metal caused by the head-on collision pushed the cab's instrument panel upward violently, catching the engineer under the chin and decapitating him.

Why had the second locomotive been on the same track? Reports say that a rail-shop employee at Boston Bar was moving the locomotive by himself at low speed and slipped off to throw a track switch, a common practice in those days. But the locomotive gathered speed and he was unable to get back on. It rolled onto the main line, uncontrolled, leading to the fatal accident down the line.

Tales of trouble, and often terror, on the tracks are not common, but accidents do happen and when they do, the outcomes are often brutal.

CABOOSE ON THE LOOSE

IT WAS 1947, the night before New Year's Eve. The freezing air was still, except for a hint of a morning wind. An unoccupied caboose sat alone and motionless in the stillness. But not for long.

At the train track summit of Judah Hill, in Peace River country and high above the Peace River Bridge, a brakeman for Northern Alberta Railways (NAR), Bill Lee, conductor Scotty Hall, and crewmates shivered in the −34°C (−29°F) cold. They parked a short train of boxcars they had pulled to the summit, where it would wait to be joined with other cars brought up on a subsequent trip. When they had arrived, the caboose was sitting uncoupled and untended, while the boxcars were set on a siding. Long trains were understandably too heavy for the demanding incline of the 2.6 percent grade. The train to be hauled up was reduced to workable lengths in order to ensure safe passage along the eleven kilometres (seven miles) of steep track leading up from the river's bridge below. The process, known as "doubling," was time-consuming though necessary in order to ease the tonnage per train to a manageable amount, therefore necessitating two or more trips to bring an entire train to the summit.

As morning neared, the crew stomped their feet and hugged themselves to keep warm as they prepared to return down the hill and pick up the next section of freight that awaited them. When all the other cars had been moved up the hill to the summit, they would be rejoined into one long consist before heading east toward Edmonton.

To facilitate parking their night shift's first group of boxcars, Bill Lee had earlier uncoupled caboose No. 13002 and left it stable on flat rails. A coal-oil lamp provided a comforting glow through the caboose windows, easing the night's blackness to a welcoming grey and the snow's white to soft amber.

Near the base of Judah Hill and far below this NAR working crew, the railway agent's two-storey building was coming to life. The pre-dawn hours felt bitterly cold. Agent Swanny Swanson began the early part of his workday moving from the upstairs residence to the agent's office on the first floor, where the stove's warmth made him the envy of outside labourers. His jacket was off and to the side. Near him was the lit lantern he used for light and signalling. Swanson's current job with NAR took him along the railway, providing temporary relief for regular agents who were away tending to business or personal matters. On post near the Peace River Bridge that morning, he had every reason to feel it was the beginning of another predictable shift in his railway life. Instead, it would be a day of near misses, averted tragedy, and the start of a cover-up. His morning calm was about to be shattered.

On the plateau far above Swanson, the stationary caboose suddenly began to move. Some would later say the train had inadvertently nudged it during shunting. Others speculated that the flat rails on which it rested actually had a slight slope impossible for the workers to have noticed in the dark. Either way, the untethered caboose found a friend in gravity. It broke an ill-set brake and slipped down into the dark.

As the caboose rolled, the astonished crew watched helplessly. The car's gathering speed quickly outreached their ability to stop it and reset the handbrake. Then it headed downhill. Looks of horror were swapped as their errant coach disappeared from sight. They knew it could not go far without falling off the tracks and into certain, twisted ruin. They did not for a moment imagine that it could careen westward for eleven kilometres (seven miles) in nearly as many minutes, repeatedly corner without toppling, and move ever more rapidly toward the town once called Peace River Crossing and known at that time, and today, simply as Peace River.

Between the town and the fast-tracking caboose rushing down Judah Hill was the fifty-year-old Peace River Bridge. In a reasonable gesture of cost saving, vehicles and trains used the same bridge, one or another at a time passing over its narrow surface. Trains had priority, and their passage always occurred with advance roadway signal lights set to warn of their pending arrival. Such indicators would clear the bridge of any vehicles or pedestrians. With no warning lights showing that morning, taxi driver Earl Boyd of course thought it was safe to drive across the 518-metre (1,700-foot) bridge. Boyd swung his car up onto the trestle's railway/roadway as he headed north over the river, unaware of the threat swiftly bearing down the hillside behind him.

The caboose, its metallic flanges squeaking loudly, seemed destined to wreck itself along with whatever it smashed into. Its course was set to hurtle across the bridge and right into Boyd, who heard not a thing.

Someone was listening, though. The oncoming sound of steel wheels on steel tracks is one that railway men usually welcome. Often, it brings fellow workers and camaraderie—perhaps coffee time and shared stories. But to Agent Swanson that morning, there was something dangerously unfamiliar about the metallic screeches approaching his building. Through the ice-covered windowpane, he saw the loose caboose reel by at nearly a hundred kilometres (sixty miles) an hour.

Bolting through the door with his jacket in one hand and the lantern in the other, Swanson ran downhill. He saw the taxi's lights as it crossed the bridge below, where the flying caboose would surely sweep the tracks in a matter of seconds. His heart thumped with the rhythm of a runaway train. Swanson watched helplessly as the tilting caboose held tight to the curving rails, righted itself, and, still gaining speed, tipped onto the bridge.

As Boyd neared the other end of the bridge, his headlights shone on the water tank built beside the tracks. He steered his car off the bridge and onto one of the town's roads, completely unaware of the oncoming train car. The rushing caboose whooshed by his bumper, missing it by a moment.

Disaster was not yet averted. The caboose, keeping on the tracks, headed straight from the bridge and up an incline, approaching the outer township of Roma. The rise of track slowed and stopped the caboose; it remained stationary for a speck of time. Then it reversed direction, once more picking up speed, its wheel flanges again screaming. With the caboose now racing toward the bridge from the other side, Swanson made it to a point where he could warn away car traffic at his end, freeing up the bridge.

When the runaway crossed back over the bridge, it sped by Swanson at such a rate that he dared not jump on board. It started up the lower part of Judah Hill toward the NAR's station house. When he realized what was going to happen next, the railroader decided to make his move. He gauged the caboose. He watched its rise and saw it drop momentum. The grade's steepness brought it to a momentary stop. Then, just as suddenly, it began to move: another yo-yo descent, heading back toward the bridge, taking on speed with each length of track. Years later, Swanson recalled his actions: "I climbed on at eight miles an hour and tied it down with the handbrake." It stopped.

Pulling open the caboose door to see if anyone was in there, Swanson gulped for air as smoke pushed by him. A smoldering fire burst into flame. The train lantern had tumbled out of its latched holding during the whiplash ride down Judah Hill. Swanson grabbed a burning mattress and flung it outside into the snow. It took the flames with it, saving the caboose from an engulfing blaze.

When he finally made his way once more into the caboose, nothing was where it should have been. Everything had been tossed about in heaps or strewn across the floorboards, "Except," Swanson said, "the stove, which was bolted to the floor."

Coming down the tracks from above on a slowly reversing engine, the crew who'd been in charge of the caboose looked lost and defeated. From their vantage point, they did not have the river's bridge in their line of sight and had not been aware how far the loose caboose had travelled. They had been crawling around the hill near the track, looking for wreckage, certain their lost car would be found flung off the tracks in twisted and shattered disarray. They were astonished to find it upright, with Swanson in the doorway and a smouldering mattress at its side.

With no one hurt and the caboose stable, relief set in. Guilt replaced fear, and a new worry replaced terror. Adrenalin and irrational thinking took over. Rapidly assessing their good luck, one of the crew said, "I think we'll try and cover this up." They kept the news from railway officials for six weeks.

In train towns, such stories spread faster than a mattress fire. Town folk all knew of the incident within hours. By midday, the calamity and near disaster was on its way to healthy embellishment, and no one could contain it. But there was hope the secret would remain a local one. Swanson went so far as to dissuade the newspaper from covering the escapade. In the editorial silence and community cooperation that followed, no one at head office in Edmonton knew anything about the company's narrow escape from human and financial tragedy.

Everything was fine until a month and a half later, when the NAR's general manager, J.M. MacArthur, made a trip from Edmonton to Peace River. He was the featured speaker at the local board of trade dinner meeting and was seated with local dignitaries and their spouses. In an innocent turn of conversation toward the evening's end, the bank manager's wife, who was next to MacArthur, said, "It was sure funny what happened to the caboose."

One errant line about one errant caboose, and an investigation was begun.

Since the melee happened on Swanny Swanson's watch and he did not communicate it to his superiors, responsibility and subsequent discipline fell mostly on his shoulders. Following a report on the mishap, Swanson received an NAR envelope containing a reprimand for how he had conducted himself in the aftermath of the events. Inside the folder, he found a company form docking him ten demerit marks, a clear cost to him for not disclosing the situation. Chastised, he opened the envelope's second formal document. This one granted him fifteen merit points for bringing the loose caboose to a stop.

Journalist Stuart Adams interviewed Swanson before his death in 2008 and wrote about the caboose adventure for *Classic Trains* magazine. Adams quotes Swanson: "I claim to be the only railroader who got disciplined and rewarded for the same incident."

EIGHTEEN SECONDS TO HELL

AS DAWN BROKE on Saturday, February 8, 1986, it was a chilly
−13°C (9°F) in Jasper, Alberta. VIA Rail passenger Kenneth Cuttle
prepared to reboard Train No. 4 after a sixty-minute stop on its way
from Vancouver eastbound to Edmonton. He'd strolled around the
station to stretch his legs and explore the town. Now, as he headed
for the dome car, he invited a fellow passenger, a young man from
England, to join him. "The view and the sunrise will be worth it," he
promised, as they sat down at the front of the car.

At 7:15 a.m., Train 4 left the station for Edmonton with
two experienced, well-rested engineers in the lead locomotive:
fifty-three-year-old Emil Miller, who was at the controls, and fifty-
seven-year-old Mike Peleshaty. At 8:20, the train arrived at Hinton,
where, as was their routine, the men exchanged positions. At Pedley,
the next station, the dispatcher arranged for the switch at Dalehurst
to open, which would enable the train to pass.

The 114 cars loaded with grain, steel pipes, and dangerous cargo
that made up CN freight train No. 413 left Edmonton at 1:55 a.m.,
westbound for Vancouver. At 6:40, it passed through Edson, Alberta,
now with forty-eight-year-old engineer Jack Hudson at the controls.
He'd already been up for several hours, and, having had just three
and a half hours of sleep, was tired. Technically, the train hadn't
even stopped at Edson, which was where incoming and outgoing
crews exchanged positions. In an illegal technique known as "taking
the train on the fly," the train was slowed just enough to enable the

Kenneth Cuttle helped rescue passengers in the Hinton rail crash. ELAINE DOUGAN

exchanges, in order to avoid starting the long freight train from a standstill on an uphill grade.

Train 413 departed from Medicine Lodge (near Hargwen), arriving at Mile 156.5 at about 8:30 a.m. Near Mile 169, thirty-three-year-old conductor Wayne Smith, looking ahead from his post of duty in the cupola of his caboose, tried (as he habitually did) to call the crew on the locomotive to ask how things were going. Although he called at least twice, there was no response. This was not unusual, since the terrain west of Mile 165 was well known as an area of spotty radio communication. About 610 metres (2,000 feet) before the train got to the Dalehurst home signal (close to Mile 172.9), three vertical red lights, meaning "stop," would have been visible to the engineer and brakeman. For some reason, the engineer did not obey.

Meanwhile, on Train No. 4, Kenneth Cuttle noticed something unusual but wasn't worried. "I saw lights flickering in the trees quite a way off, and I assumed it was another train coming toward us, but

I also assumed incorrectly that there were two lines and it was going to pass," he recalled. He also remembered seeing red signals east of the lead locomotive.

As Train No. 4 approached Dalehurst and was in sight of the home signal, the signal changed to red/red/red as a result of Train No. 413 entering the Dalehurst switch at its east end.

At 8:40.34, Train No. 413 arrived at Dalehurst, and its crew ran through a switch governing its entry onto a single-track section. In the dome car, Kenneth Cuttle saw that the approaching train was on the same track. "He's on our track!" he yelled. One can only imagine the terror that ensued for the next eighteen seconds, with the two trains on the same track and within sight of each other.

At 8:40.52, Trains 4 and 413 collided head-on in a hellish nightmare of death and destruction.

Conductor Smith, sitting in the caboose's cupola on Train 413, felt the emergency brakes automatically apply on impact. He looked ahead into the horror of a gigantic fireball. Thinking that the dangerous goods had exploded, he sent a message to the front-end crew, advising them to stay away from those cars. But it was too late. The train had stopped moving.

The impact of the collision had been devastating and horrific. Cuttle later said,

> Fortunately, the damage that was coming like a tidal wave our way stopped just before the dome car. There were five of us in it: myself, the young Englishman, a woman (who was sleeping), and two other men. We were all thrown right over backwards to the end of the carriage. The glass in the dome roof was cracked. I jumped on a chair and pushed myself headfirst through the glass, and sat there, half in, half out, with my legs dangling below. I pulled the woman up through this "avenue of escape" that I'd smashed out. I yelled at the others to "Get cracking and get out

Aerial view of the Hinton crash. SUN MEDIA

now!" We all got out, and then jumped—nearly fourteen feet [four metres] to the ground.

I was just in my shirt sleeves, cold and dazed. I lay there for a few moments and then I heard cries for help, moans and groans. It was terrible to listen to. Suddenly, a rail worker shouted, "Clear the train, it's going to blow!"

Then there was an explosion; anybody trapped in the train was burned to death immediately. The shouting and screaming stopped.

It was like a mini atom bomb. There was a huge pall of black smoke. There were massive, long steel pipes... everything you could imagine was airborne. Tonnage, up there in the sky, coming toward us, and fortunately it stopped right before the dome car. All the other coaches were crushed and flattened. Everybody in there had no chance all.

Twenty-three people perished in the Hinton crash, including the head-end crews of both trains, one passenger in the dome car, and eighteen in the day coach. Seventy-one others were injured. The collision was the worst ever in Alberta and the worst in Canada since 1947.

Within twenty minutes, the RCMP arrived. An officer found Kenneth Cuttle shivering and bleeding from the head and put him in his car to keep warm. Eventually, Cuttle was taken to a nearby lumber camp, where good medical assistance was available. A nurse removed many pieces of glass from his head. Amazingly, he was free of any other physical injuries. The fellow passengers he helped to safety were treated at the camp, too, and were not seriously hurt.

Cuttle's son drove from his home in Edmonton to pick up his dad. The next day, Cuttle was stormed by the media, as he was the only available eyewitness. The same day, VIA Rail arranged a voucher for Cuttle to buy some clothes. VIA Rail later gave him $3,500 in total compensation. The company also supplied him with a car to drive back to his home in Victoria. Even on-board the ferry from Tsawwassen the media peppered him with questions.

Within two days, the governor-general appointed the Honourable Justice René Paul Foisy of the Court of Queen's Bench of Alberta to inquire into the collision. Kenneth Cuttle was the only surviving eyewitness passenger to appear at the inquiry.

Among other things, Foisy's report found that, amazingly enough, brakes were not applied on the freight train, even though the trains were clearly visible to each other for several seconds. He determined that the signals were functioning properly, and that no mechanical problems contributed to the accident.

The disaster, he said, was directly caused by the failure of Train 413 to obey signals requiring it stop, and by its crew's decision to run through the switch that governed its entry onto a single track.

Beyond that, Foisy identified "railroad culture" as a contributing factor to the collision. That culture was characterized by crews who were willing to "gain standing" by demonstrating endurance working long hours without adequate rest. Apparently, Engineer Hudson and two other crew members had not had adequate sleep the night before.

"Railroad culture" also manifested in a disregard for safety—by both CN employees and management. Employees were reluctant to report fellow employees' violations, health issues, or other problems. Management, it seemed, failed to intervene in long-standing violations.

Some may wonder why CN even allowed Hudson to work, since he had a history of performance and safety violations. He had accumulated fifty demerit points as of 1983; an accumulation of sixty points would have resulted in automatic dismissal. Although management warned him about accumulating more points, records showed there had been more violations, but no points were ever assessed.

One mystery remaining unsolved was whether Train 413's operator had altered the functioning of the deadman's pedal, a safety device in the locomotive that the engineer's foot must keep depressed, otherwise the train will stop automatically. With this feature, even if the crew had, for whatever reason, become incapacitated, the engineer's foot would have come away from the pedal in enough time to avoid a collision. Boredom for long periods of time and the discomfort of keeping a foot on the pedal sometimes led engineers to place a heavy object on the pedal to bypass its function. Because Train 413's lead locomotive was destroyed, it was impossible to ascertain if the pedal had in fact been bypassed. Anyone with knowledge of railway operations was stunned. Why hadn't CN installed a superior safety device, known as a Reset Safety Control, in Train 413's lead locomotive? (There was such a device in the other train's locomotive.) This control requires the crew to push a button at regular intervals, otherwise brakes will be applied.

Finally, how was it that Conductor Smith's attempts to reach the head-end crew on two different radios failed, yet they worked when he spoke with the dispatcher immediately after the collision?

Looking back at age ninety, Kenneth Cuttle credits his years as a former marine commando in the Second World War—in which he endured stressful situations that required quick responses—with helping him react as he did and saving four lives. "Within a week of the collision, the president of VIA Rail phoned to thank me for what I did," he says. "They gave me a first-class lifetime pass, but what I really wanted and never received was official recognition from the government."

BRIDGES AND BARGES
DON'T MIX WELL

JUNE 2, 1999, proved to be a fateful day for a bridge and a barge known as *Rivtow 901*.

The Mission Railway Bridge was the first bridge built across the Lower Fraser River, in 1891. It was originally made of wood, but within two decades, staged replacements had converted it to a steel-and-concrete structure. It provided an important link between the US and the CPR line that ran along the north shore of the river. Mission was selected as an ideal site for connecting a line from the American town of Sumas because of the proximity of the US border, just a few kilometres south. Until the New Westminster Bridge was built in 1904, the Mission Railway Bridge was the only rail link with the south. Today, dozens of trains cross the bridge in either direction every day, including consists from CP, CN, VIA Rail, and the Rocky Mountaineer.

The bridge sports a swing span toward the south shore to facilitate the passage of river traffic too tall to slip under the structure. The river is a few dozen metres deep here, depending on the time of year and whether the spring freshet is raising the water. On the north side of the bridge, the famous "Mission Gauge" displays the height of the river at all times during the year. The Fraser River rises and falls daily as tides back up the flow where it enters the Strait of Georgia, part of the Salish Sea, some seventy kilometres (forty-three miles) to the west. The tidal effect travels all the way up to Mission, and the Mission Gauge is seen as a critical indicator of the danger of flooding in May and June each year. Crucial elements for mariners navigating under the bridge include the cycle of tides and the time of year; if the freshet is in full flow and the tides have pushed the river levels up, greater care is needed when approaching the bridge because there is less space between the surface of the water and the bottom of the bridge.

The bridge tender opens the swing span if an approaching vessel requests it. In early days, a horse named Charlie controlled the opening of the span by walking in a circle around a capstan. Later, electric motors took over those responsibilities and Charlie retired to a pasture nearby.

On June 2, 1999, the river was in freshet. River tug *Sheena M* was dispatched to Mission to deliver an empty wood-chip barge and then return to Annacis Island, near New Westminster, with a loaded barge, the *Rivtow 901*. This process was routine, but while the tug's master had navigated the Mission Bridge hundreds of times, he had last done so almost a decade earlier, and that wasn't during freshet.

The trip upriver passed without incident, and the empty barge was delivered to the Meeker Cedar Mill, a few hundred metres east of the bridge. The *Rivtow 901* was taken under tow for the return journey, bearing a load of chips weighing around 2,100 tons. The barge itself was a typical Rivtow unit, a steel barge designed to hold wood chips in bulk. Steel bulwarks surrounded the deck to a height of almost five metres, each side reinforced by steel stanchions on the outside. Tug and barge left the Meeker site shortly after midnight, approaching the bridge from the east. The captain called the bridge tender to ask for the span to be opened to allow the tug's mast to pass. With the Mission Gauge reading just over four and a half metres (fifteen feet), the opening was needed. The master and his deckhand noticed that the lights on the bridge seemed dim. Atmospheric conditions were perfect, so fog or mist were not issues. As they approached the bridge, the captain felt the current strengthen, and he compensated by adjusting his throttle and his helm to ensure both the *Sheena M* and the *Rivtow 901*, following about fifteen metres (fifty feet) behind the tug, would navigate under the bridge safely. The barge stayed in deeper water and moved toward the swing span. The *Sheena M* had passed safely, but the feel from the tow wire told the master the barge had not. Meanwhile, the scream of breaking wood and tearing metal heard by the deckhand confirmed the worst: the barge being towed by the tug had run into the Mission Railway Bridge. Neither the master nor the deckhand realized that the damage to the bridge would put it out of commission for weeks.

The master quickly called the bridge tender, who was now stranded on the open swing span, to make sure he was all right. He was, but the swing span wasn't.

The *Sheena M*'s crew tied up the *Rivtow 901* just downstream from the bridge, and the tug returned to pick up the stranded bridge tender, but he'd already left via water taxi. The swing span was tipping precariously in the midnight darkness, and he hadn't wanted to wait for the tug's return.

Dawn's light revealed the extent of the damage. The *Sheena M* lost its mast when it was caught in cable that had broken loose when the swing span was struck. The barge's metal sides had been bent and buckled for about six metres (twenty feet), but beyond that, the hull was fine and very little of the cargo had been lost in the river. But the bridge told a different story. The bridge structure that sat to the upstream side of the span took the brunt of the collision, and the resulting deflection knocked the swing span from its pedestal, and it was out of alignment by around four metres (thirteen feet). The span had then teetered over the damaged base. The bridge was out of service, and all rail traffic using it came to halt.

The Mission Rail Bridge tips precariously over the Fraser River the morning after it was struck by the *Rivtow 901.* **TRANSPORTATION SAFETY BOARD OF CANADA**

It was almost a month before repairs to the swing span were completed; in the meantime, rail traffic was rerouted over bridges in the Fraser Canyon or at New Westminster. This put stress on the CN line south of the river, which had to absorb traffic to and from the US that normally moved straight north across the bridge to hook up with the main CPR line on the north side. River traffic under the bridge was affected as well because the span was sitting across the channel it would normally use.

The final report from the Transportation Safety Board of Canada determined "that bridge lighting on the Fraser River is inconsistent with respect to nominal range." More lights were added to the bridge structure to ensure it was more visible. Repairs to the damaged upstream portion of the swing span proceeded, and the existing wood section that had been crushed was replaced with steel. The nose of the pier was lengthened. And more training for crew members navigating the span was implemented.

The bridge had suffered other accidents. The flood of 1948 took away a twenty-five-metre (eighty-two-foot) section, and when a span and pier collapsed in 1955, repairs took over a year. Other Fraser River bridges have suffered from similar collisions with more than four dozen occurring on spans that cross the river downstream from Mission in the past quarter century.

The sound of train horns as consists cross the bridge are a staple in Mission—crossings from either side require horn signals—but things grew very quiet for a month in 1999 when residents found out that bridges and barges sometimes don't mix well.

WORKING ON
THE RAILROAD

ACOUPLE OF OKANAGAN boys tour a construction site of the Kettle Valley Railway in 1915 and get to know some of the characters. A Vancouver Islander invents a railway warning signal horn that becomes an iconic, nostalgic sound. And a team of locomotive buffs lovingly rebuilds a classic engine that today attracts thousands of steam-era fans.

◄ The legendary 3716 locomotive runs along the Kettle Valley Railway line near Summerland, British Columbia, evoking a bygone era with its vintage coaches for passengers. **KETTLE VALLEY STEAM RAILWAY**

BUILDING THE KETTLE
VALLEY RAILROAD
A Boy's-eye View

As fifteen-year-old boys living in Summerland, BC, Ted Logie and his friend Bunny Merrill were intrigued by the construction of the Kettle Valley Railway in 1914–15, in particular the section above Naramata, on the east side of Okanagan Lake. Logie later wrote about many of his boyhood adventures in Ted Tells (Okanagan) Tales, *published in 1967. This is an abridged version of the chapter "Tunnel Camp." Nellie and Slim were two camp dogs.*

WHEN RAILWAY CONSTRUCTION work started back of West Summerland, it caused quite a flutter of excitement among us kids. There was considerable rock work involved, which meant mostly hand drilling, although some outfits did have compressors for air drills. There were always satisfactory explosions taking place, clouds of smoke and dust marking the spot for the eye to catch, sometimes long before the sound of the blast reached the ears.

Some of us did a little cautious investigating on the occasional Saturday, but as the work was well spread out and the blasting was almost a regular occurrence, kids were considered too much of an added risk and our duties as construction inspectors were almost always curtailed, by request, and the general impression began to be felt that we weren't really needed, especially after being repeatedly told by numerous straw bosses to "get the hell out of here."

Bunny and I planned a visit afield, a trip to the Big Tunnel, well above Naramata. We could see the occasional sign of blasting all along the construction, indication of general activity then in progress. Dad was a right-of-way agent for the railway company and knew the general layout of the proposed track. There were to be two switch-backs, and one turn was to be completed inside a tunnel that was to be over 1,800 feet [550 metres] long—this point of turning to be almost directly above Naramata. This is where Bunny and I decided to go, crossing the lake on the first ferry on a Saturday morning, then hiking up the mountain to our objective. We didn't know anything about roads or trails, but that didn't matter; we would pack lunches, and who could get lost with the lake in plain view?

We reached the tunnel construction as planned, although we didn't locate any beaten path to follow. We struck straight up the mountain and were guided by the sound of blasting directly above us. By the time we got there, hunger had arrived with us and we began to look for a favourable spot to eat lunch. We were going to begin this enjoyable pastime, when a tough-looking character, with a voice to match, asked, "What are you kids doing here?" "We're starting to eat our lunch," we replied. We were informed, "You can't eat lunch here, come on." He led the way toward camp, two rather perplexed kids following dutifully at his heels. He went straight to the office and walked in. "I found these kids going to eat their lunch out on the job," he informed a man who was doing some paperwork at a desk. "They should know better than that," he said, looking at us, and that was the first time I saw George Harmont, the man who later was to become my brother-in-law.

We were still puzzled. Nothing had been said to us as to what we were supposed to do, when suddenly the cookhouse triangle sounded and everybody moved, fast. With a hurried "come on," our first acquaintance, who turned out to be Lou Bacher, of the firm of Bacher and Harmont, led the way, and soon we were seated at the bosses' table, eating as fast as we could, but not nearly fast enough to keep up with the average construction worker, whose usual time from "sit down" to "get up" was twelve minutes. Those at the bosses' table took a little longer. They included the engineers on the job, the timekeeper, George, and Lou. There were a couple of spare places to sit intruders such as ourselves. Everyone finished before Bunny and I had reached the dessert stage, and Lou, on leaving, gave a parting injunction to the flunky waiting on the table, "See that these kids get lots of pie."

Bill, the cook, came and sat down with us before we left to pass the time of day and ask us where we came from, but mostly, I think, to have a quiet cup of coffee and cigarette after his work of feeding the hungry crew. Another meal had been completed, and he had an hour off before he started all over again. We thanked him for the meal, especially the pumpkin pie, of which, for once, we had eaten more than enough.

We went back to the office, where Lou Bacher informed us he was going out on the job and would we care to come along. Would we! After being chased off construction projects over at Summerland, to arrive at this one where kids were even fed was too good to be true, but I must say in all fairness that when we were told to "scram" off those workings, it was for our own protection—they didn't want any kids around who might get hurt.

Lou Bacher was a rough-looking man. He had started out as a youngster, followed construction work, mostly railroad, all his life, working as a flunky to begin with and gradually worked his way up. George had the book knowledge, although he too had acquired his share of the general know-how, and the two men worked well together.

Lou showed us all over. They were working from both portals of the tunnel, what they called the East and the West Approaches, and to meet the time limit in their contract, they had broken through

Dinky engine (a small locomotive) with load. TED LOGIE PHOTO COLLECTION

at the centre and were working both ways from the break-through, thus giving them four faces where work was going on.

At the East Approach, there was a good-sized gravel bank that had to be taken out, and they hoped to move this with a large charge of black powder that was to be placed in a coyote hole and exploded. A coyote hole was bigger than a badger hole and was really a small tunnel drilled into the gravel bank. The charge was to be detonated with wires, this being done at a safe distance from the scene of the blast.

The following Sunday night, about 9:30, Lou said, "come on" and we waited for George, and the three of us went down to the cookhouse, where the night cook was working. He did all the pastry baking and was just taking doughnuts out of the hot grease. We rolled them in icing sugar, and they sure were good.

Next morning, George had some book work to do, so Lou, Slim, Nellie, and I went out to the East Approach. I watched the "dump" horse hauling rock and gravel in dump cars on a light railway. Lou went into the workings, as he said he had to "raise hell with some Swedes." Nellie and Slim were soon chasing chipmunks. I started to drive the horse, but there wasn't much to it. The horse knew what to do, and it was just a case of "giddy-up" and "whoa." Dumping the waste was harder, though: the cars tipped sideways, and sometimes the rocks got jammed and had to be pried loose. The guy that was on that job was glad of a rest, but I didn't work too long. Sometimes a dump car went over the bank, and Lou said it took a lot of cussing to get it back.

The haul gradually got longer, and eventually they got a Dinky engine to do the hauling, it was a gas-and-diesel affair and could haul about four or five cars at a time. Bill the timekeeper ran that. Once he put it over the [bank into the] dump and he told me that after Lou had finished with him, his ears tingled for a week. It was pretty badly dented but still ran when they got it back up,

Workers and friends at Tunnel Camp. Front row, left to right: Jack Logie; his wife, Ruby; Thea Mason. Back row, left to right: Bill (the timekeeper); Lou Bacher; George (possibly George Harmont); Ted Logie; George Christ. TED LOGIE PHOTO COLLECTION

and after the smoke of the cussing had died down a bit, George said he thought it ran better and Lou said it should, it had more experience now.

After about the third trip up to the Tunnel Camp, Lou said I would have to get my picture taken to show the family what I did when I left home, and he rigged up a poker game. Bill was behind the counter pretending to be taking a swig out of a bottle, and on the table was all the big money that Lou could rustle, mostly twenty-dollar bills. There was a small glass of cough medicine at my side, and I was showing my hand, four aces and the joker, and raking in the pot, while George covered Lou with a six-shooter to make him behave. The picture didn't cause any commotion at home: they were wise to what I did at the Tunnel Camp and also knew by this time what Lou was liable to come up with.

That poker game almost had a very sad ending. I managed to hit that glass full of cough medicine, and it spilled over all the money on the table, nice thick, syrupy, gooey stuff. Lou washed the bills off in water and put them on the heater to dry.

Lou used to go down to the bunkhouse and sit in on the [real] poker game, and it was fairly strong medicine. Lou did fairly well, though, until George got mad and made him quit. I went down one night and was looking on, and the fellow that I was watching won a fairly big pot. He saw me there and slipped me four bits and told me to stay with it, I was bringing him luck. Sure enough, he won the next pot, and I got another four bits. Then I began to wonder what would happen if he started to lose, so I eased out of there.

The men used to play after payday until one or two of the players had cornered most of the cash in the camp. Then they would drift up to the next camp, and eventually the winners there would possibly end up in Kelowna, where a bigger game was in progress twenty-four hours a day. They might stay lucky for a while, but eventually the run of the cards would send them back [to the work site and] they would start all over again. Seemingly, that was the life they enjoyed.

ROMEO'S SNOW SLIDE

WORK ON THE Kettle Valley Railway was often dirty, dangerous, and dehydrating in the summer and deadly cold in the winter. One such cold snap hit hard in January 1935. It was a bone-chilling −37°C (−34°F) outdoors. A snow slide had hit at Romeo, one of the many Shakespearian names—including Juliet, Portia, Lear, and

Iago—bestowed along the Coquihalla Canyon by the KVR's masterful engineer Andrew McCulloch. Trainman Dick Geldreich and his crew were at Iago, intending to top up the coal in the tender before heading back up the Coquihalla River Canyon.

A plow crew used a conductor's track phone to contact the section men at Iago, warning that a big slide had hit between Romeo and Iago. Then the phone suddenly went silent. Geldreich and the others jumped out of the train and crowded into the nearby section house.

Then it started to snow. For three days and nights, it fell thick and dense, dumping more than four metres (thirteen feet) of the white stuff. Inside, the worried men huddled together. How long would they have to wait? Their only provisions were a sack of oatmeal, 2.3 kilograms (5 pounds) of meat, a few vegetables, and 90 to 135 kilograms (200 to 300 pounds) of flour. When the snow finally eased, the temperature rose. Torrential rains cascaded down the mountains for another three days and nights.

Nothing was stable; it seemed the whole countryside would slip away. A part of it did, and with a violent force, a slide slammed into the section house, bursting through the door of a lean-to kitchen and half-filling it with snow.

On the seventh day, the crew ran out of food and decided to walk uphill to Romeo. Before leaving, they tore away pieces of the section house wall and fashioned them into makeshift snowshoes, then set out on a perilous and exhausting eleven-kilometre (seven-mile) journey as they climbed their way over and around slides, tunnels, and snowsheds.

Hungry and tired, they finally reached Romeo, where a stranded merchandise train loaded with groceries greeted the bedraggled crew. (That train was later struck by an avalanche, which derailed a number of cars.) Once rejuvenated, the men started walking again, heading for the Coquihalla Summit. Halfway to Juliet, the most welcoming site emerged: a rescue snowplow sent to find them. It had been a nerve-racking eleven days—but, unlike some others, they had not lost their lives to winter's wrath along the KVR.

WHISTLING UP A WARNING

COLLIDING WITH A train can lead to disaster! An accident survived by a logging-truck driver on Vancouver Island in the 1940s led to the creation of some of the North American train-horn sounds most know and love—and a few hate—today.

The clarion call from the horn of a distant train approaching a train crossing is well known throughout the continent: two long blasts, then a short one, then another long blast as the train passes through the crossing; it's a standard sound heard everywhere rails run, but it wasn't always so. Early diesel locomotives used much simpler horns that sounded like truck horns. When that logging-truck driver moving his load near the Vancouver Island city of Nanaimo mistook the alert from an approaching train to be just another truck horn, he moved into the crossing and was hit. The accident caught the attention of a local man, Robert Swanson, who embarked on a quest to invent a new air horn.

Steam engines were phasing out in those days, and the number of diesel locomotives was increasing rapidly. Steam whistles were distinctive—there was no mistaking the sound they made. Bob Swanson had been working with steam most of his life. While he worked in local mines and mills, he upgraded his steam tickets and eventually earned his engineering degree. Along the way, he established a "whistle farm" at a remote location in the Nanaimo River valley where he could develop new signalling devices for sawmills without disturbing the neighbours.

With the logging-truck accident on his mind, Swanson tackled the development of a unique train horn sound that could never be mistaken for a truck. His first task was to analyze the sound of steam whistles, and he established the combination of five "musical notes" that created the chord made by the most common whistles. At least four different manufacturers offered horns with different sounds, some melodious, evoking the romance of rail travel and the "sound of the outward bound" (a line from a '50s hit song "The Wayward Wind"). The classic horn sequence provided an aural backdrop to many a tale told in books, songs, and movies.

In short order, Swanson had developed what he called his "five chime" horn, which he labelled the "H5," for "Hexatone 5 Chime": it was a five-note chord, thus five "chimes." A patent application followed, along with the launch of his own business, AirChime. Other horn designs and improvements followed, including the M, the P, and the K series. The last diesel whistle Swanson developed was termed "a diminished C chord" and is still in use today.

Swanson's horns caught on with many railroads, and their signature sound became commonplace across North America in the following decades. The journey from a "whistle farm" in the depths of a forest near Nanaimo to horns used on locomotives across the continent was quite a trip, but this was only one of Swanson's many accomplishments. AirChime's products supplied ferries, ships, sawmills, and, eventually, the famous "O Canada" air horn that sounds at twelve o'clock noon every day from atop the Pan Pacific Hotel at Canada Place on Vancouver's waterfront. This horn travelled on the lead locomotive of the Confederation Train, which crossed Canada during the 1967 centennial year.

Many other horns were developed by Swanson's company, with different combinations of "bells"—the actual horns—generating different notes or chords. Earlier versions could be "played" or "feathered" by individual operators, as a whistle cord was pulled with

The classic Nathan AirChime K5LA horn assembly, found on diesel locomotives across North America. Each "trumpet" delivers a different note to produce the final sound of the horn. **AMERICAN AIR HORN DISTRIBUTION COMPANY HORNBLASTERS**

varying force to allow more or less compressed air into the chambers, thus delivering different sounds. Horns these days are operated by a push switch or an automatic device that plays the appropriate crossing sequence. Some people consider more contemporary horns to be brash or harsh, lacking the melodious tones of earlier models. Since their objective is to alert motorists and pedestrians to the approach of a train, however, a more jarring sound is likely to be more effective. In any event, the lonesome wail of a train horn has been part of the North American ethos for over 150 years and is now part of our public consciousness.

Swanson operated his business in BC for decades and eventually sold it to another horn company, Nathan Manufacturing, and the product name "Nathan AirChime" became widely known. Today, AirChime is owned by Micro Precision Group and remains one of two leading North American manufacturers of train horns, the other being Leslie Controls. AirChime has been called "the industry standard," and its products remain common in the train-horn business. Other manufacturers have provided competition over the years, including Buell, Prime, and Westinghouse.

Other creations from the inventive mind of Bob Swanson include a logging-truck braking system and runaway lanes for logging trucks on hills. He was the motivating force behind the refurbishment of the Royal Hudson (2860) steam locomotive that is kept today at the West Coast Railway Heritage Park in Squamish and plied the rails along Howe Sound over many years. Swanson at one point was the chief inspector of railroads for the Province of British Columbia. And he was known as the "Bard of the Woods" for the many poems he wrote about logging, collected in four books. Swanson died in 1994, with his legacy safely intact across the world wherever railroads, ships, and mills ply their trades.

Train horns have become a public issue today. Rules and regulations require their use at all times, but communities across North America have questioned the need, particularly overnight in urban areas, where some people claim their sleep is disrupted by them. With crossing signals and controls in place in many areas, critics say the horns are redundant, and some communities have established corridors where every crossing is controlled, thus reducing the need, in their view, for warning signals. Railway companies are not convinced, and the debate continues.

Signals required by regulation and by railroad practice are consistent in North America. The "two long blasts, a short, and a long, over a period between fifteen and twenty seconds long," is the standard "call" when approaching a crossing. Other calls are used to signal the application or releasing of air brakes, to acknowledge other signals or approaching stations, and to give general warnings, as well as several other applications.

Fans of train horns abound. YouTube offers various different recordings of the many versions of train horns. The Horn and Whistle Enthusiasts Group promotes the preservation and collection of horns and whistles of various types. Some are mounted on pickup trucks as a unique signalling device. Others are just "toys for boys," operated for fun in backyards across North America. For many people, the haunting nature of a train horn in the distance evokes feelings of nostalgia, a sense of the adventure embodied in the rails that criss-cross the continent.

The birth of the AirChime train horn took place in a quiet corner of Vancouver Island because a trucker mistook the horn of an approaching train for that of another truck and lived to tell the tale. Today, no one can mistake the call of an approaching locomotive.

DELECTABLE DERAILMENT

ALAN PALM CHUCKLED as he told this story about his eastbound train pulling into Brookmere one day in the late 1940s with a refrigerator car full of beer, destined for nearby Princeton, BC. Another train was going to pick it up and deliver it to Princeton the next day, so Palm's crew went about "kicking" it onto another track. This involved the engine giving the car a short boost, and the car would be uncoupled on the fly. Alan gave the hogger (engineer) the kick signal, but the hogger was too busy waving to his family across the tracks and didn't see the signal to stop. The car got too much of a kick. An alert, frantic crew member, startled by what he saw was about to happen, jumped into action. While he was struggling and desperately applying the brake, a chain link that connected the brake to a rigging underneath the car snapped with a harsh metal twang.

The freewheeling beer car continued to rumble along and smashed into other cars already on the track. Moments later, beer gushed from the ice compartments and floor drains onto the snow. A heady half-metre-high (two-foot) foam mushroomed forth, much to the entertainment and delight of Brookmere residents, who came running with pots and pans to salvage the delectable brew.

LEAVING TOWN

CLIF CHAPMAN WORKED as a locomotive fireman throughout Alberta and BC during the last of the steam days, from 1953 to 1960. He qualified as a locomotive engineer in 1957 and shortly after—in 1960—joined the Edmonton Police Service, retiring in 1989. He rejoined the Service in 1990 as a civilian and still works there as a performance evaluator. Chapman is wise and wily, experienced, and humble. Most of all, he's a great storyteller. "There are men who went before me who should be remembered, railroaders, unique individuals, remembered by all who had the honour to work with them," says Chapman. "They were humble and without pretence—they went, they did. It's the way they *did* that I remember most." Chapman has saved those memories so he could share them.

"In the days of steam locomotives, nearly all the old-timers had nicknames," remembers Chapman. "There was Smoothy Evans, Popcorn Johnnie, Rocket Robertson, Cocky Roberts, Smiley Smith, and a host of others. But, when I let my mind wander back to those early days as a young fireboy [fledgling fireman], two names leap from the smoke and cinders—Jack O'Brien and Fred Oakley."

It was 1953, and Chapman was working out of the Hanna, Alberta, terminal. Later, he worked out of every terminal in the western region—from Hanna to Prince Rupert to Vancouver and everywhere in between. But it was Hanna where he got his start. Engines were fired with coal in those days. If you were lucky, you fired an engine with a mechanical stoker; but for him, on the spare board, it usually meant hand firing—shovelling ten to fifteen tons of coal each way over the subdivision. (Engine crews were assigned by seniority to regular, scheduled runs. Those with lesser seniority worked the "spare board.") Chapman loved it. In his spare time, he often went down to the station to watch the passenger trains come in—or more correctly—leave. He called it "an unimaginable thrill to stand on the platform, watching and listening as one of those beauties left town." The other attraction for him was knowing that those steaming lovelies were oil burners—no coal, no sweat: the firemen kept them hot without leaving their seat. (*Continued on page 109.*)

TALKIN' TRAIN TALK

TRAIN LINGO is a language unto itself. Many of its curious terms were brought over from Britain, imported from the US, or created by Canadian railroad workers. There's a dictionary's worth of slang and clever sayings that set the railroader apart from other industries, though expressions used in one rail community that may not be recognized in another. That's because there are many phrases and monikers particular to a regional area or individual train companies.

Railroad workers inspecting the rolling stock have been "carmen" or "car knockers" or, as a group, "car toads." Engineers or drivers have been nicknamed "hoggers" or "hogheads," though a novice has sometimes been a "piglet." Either way, in some jurisdictions such a position necessitated a "monkey" to "grease the pig" or "oil the engine." The brakeman has likely gone as a "brakie" or a "shack." Back before machines laid tracks, those who did so by their labour were often called "gandy dancers," meant in a flattering way and thought to come from their deft "dancing" moves as they worked, often to song, and using a measuring bar to ensure standard rail widths, a tool referenced as a "gandy."

A "fireboy" was an apprentice to a fireman, hoping to earn the more senior designation of a "bakehead." (A fireman stoked the fire in a steam engine). In the early days of steam locomotives, one of them would use a "banjo" to shovel coal, a reflection of the lifter's design being akin to the musical instrument. If their tossing of coal missed the fire door and spilled about, they were said to "throw away the diamonds."

If there was a stowaway aboard a freight train, perhaps a hobo or hitchhiker, they'd be classed as a "boxcar tourist." However, a railroad worker riding on a pass was a "dead head." Railway executives were, unflatteringly, "brass hats."

"Slaves" isn't a reference to mistreated people but to a remotely controlled set of helper locomotives marshalled into a train consist at a prescribed position. A "hot box" is not to be confused with a tool chest or storage place but should be seen as a wheel bearing that had overheated.

Safety for railroads is always of paramount importance, and to avoid a fatigued engineer falling asleep, losing attention or—perish the thought—dying while driving, there have been preventative mechanisms such as a "deadman's throttle," "deadman's pedal," or "deadman's button" that, if not stringently attended to, forced the train to stop.

Not all terminology resonates today, examples being old terms for small steam engines such as "peanut roaster," "coffee pot," or "tea kettle."

Rail fans are not exempt from mockery; their unbridled enthusiasm for trainspotting earned them the monikers "frothers" or "foamers."

Structures in rail yards earned nicknames such as "beehive" for a multi-purpose building or "buzzard's roost" for an office. Where the crew slept might be known as the "bunkhouse" or "rampasture" (the latter being a term for quarters for unmarried men). "Red onion" frequently designated the dining place. Waitresses often acknowledged the term "beanery queens" when working in a restaurant setup known as a "beanery." A railroader could order up "a string of flats and a tank car of oil" and be served hotcakes and syrup. Poached eggs over toast became "two on a raft." A day's leftovers served as the night shift's "graveyard stew."

Today, one hears "consist" to identify a group of cars or coaches that, along with the engine, form the "train set." In some parlance, a "rainbow consist" identifies a series of three or more engines, each with a different corporate-branded theme that create a colourful if uneven sight when hooked together.

While cabooses are less frequently seen today, a caboose (also known as the "brain box," "crummie," or "van") was part of freight trains but seldom part of passenger trains.

If you overheard someone talking about "strawberry patches," it could be the attractive hind-end night lights, called markers, on a caboose or on the trailing end of the last car of a passenger train. The term also applied to the clusters of red lights seen when entering Toronto's Union Station as observed from the cab of the locomotive.

The phrase "walking the dog" referred to a freight train moving so fast (perhaps quickly enough that it would be called a "ball of fire") that its cars swayed, in nerve-racking fashion, side to side and back again. What you do not want to hear is, "We're on the ground," or "We're in the weeds," as those terms mean a train has jumped the tracks, or derailed.

The term "Pacific Class 4-6-2 locomotive" hints at a whole new vocabulary. Steam locomotives are identified by the number of leading, driving, and trailing wheels that they have. This comes from a classification system developed by Frederick Methvan Whyte, a mechanical engineer. Yet most varieties carry their own names. For instance, a 4-6-4 is a Hudson, while a 4-8-4 in Canada is a Northern, and a 4-6-2 is a Pacific. A 0-4-0 is a Four Coupled, but a 0-4-0T is a "tank engine," one that carries its water tank over the top of the boiler, or in a side tank rather than in a "tender" (a supply car) behind it.

Not all train talk is of the human variety: locomotives speak for themselves constantly. Those endearing train horns we hear tell a story or share a warning. The most common is heard every time a train approaches a crossing: two long blasts, one short, and another long blast as the locomotive passes through the crossing—one good reason it's important to know your train talk!

Chapman dreamed of the day he would get called to take one of those high-stepping white-tired oil burners out of town. He watched the two regular hogheads (engineers), Fred Oakley and Jack O'Brien, mount those steeds and take them snorting and cracking into the night—Fred to the east, heading for Kindersley, Saskatchewan, and Jack heading west for Calgary.

If you were uptown in Hanna, you were only about three city blocks from the main-line steel. And, if you were there when Jack left town, you knew who was leaving. On a cold winter night, those exhausts from the stack of a Pacific Class 4-6-2 locomotive under Jack's hand brought the town to its collective feet. The sound exploded like cannon fire off the grain elevators and every building in town. The "rails" (railroad workers) walking down the street would grin at each other and say, "There goes Jack!" *No one* left town like Jack. Chapman waited. One day, he would be in that cab with Jack and they'd do it together.

Fred Oakley was a quieter guy, but he was smooth. He had a calm manner and a quiet, steady hand on the throttle. Chapman's first run with Fred was to Kindersley on an oil-burning Pacific Class steamer. He couldn't believe they were paying him to sit there and fire this beauty, charging through the night mile after mile, thrill after thrill. Fred was very kind and respectful toward his new fireboy, not always the case with senior engineers, and he taught Chapman a lot without ever really saying anything. Chapman says, "He was the type of person you respected from the start; you paid attention and you learned."

The tough part about being a spare-board fireman and the new kid on the block was not knowing the track. Every little dip and grade affected the demand for steam and the way you fired the engine. Train orders and timetables were an equal responsibility for all crew members, and you had to be alert at all times to your position on the subdivision and the exact time you should be there.

The trip east to Kindersley was a cakewalk, and after a good night's sleep, Chapman looked forward to a night run back to Hanna. He was naïve enough to think it would be just another easy one. They whistled off at 10:55 p.m. and were soon flying through the darkened countryside. They had a scheduled meet with No. 10 at Excel and No. 896 at Cereal. On they raced past Youngstown, heading for Hanna. Then it happened—ground fog! Chapman had never seen anything so sudden or so complete. One minute he was eyeballing the curving track ninety-one metres (one hundred yards) ahead, and the next he was looking at the perfect outline of the handrails on the front of the engine—and nothing more.

The hair went up on the back of Chapman's neck, and he shot a quick look at Fred Oakley. There Oakley sat, the picture of perfect serenity, calmly stroking his watch and looking at the outline of the handrails on *his* side—seemingly oblivious to the fact that they were exploding through the night going eighty kilometres (fifty miles) per hour on a 192,777-kilogram (425,000-pound) locomotive, pulling a thousand tons of coaches and passengers over rails they couldn't even see. Chapman whipped out his own watch. "Where the hell are we?" his mind screamed. This was train-order country—no safety measures like an automatic block system, no warning lights: you had to run on schedule, to the second, or risk a head-on or tail-ender because you screwed up.

Chapman recalls, "The fog waved up in front of the engine like a giant hand was flipping a blanket." Frantically, he tried to catch a glimpse of a mile marker so he could compare it to his timecard and watch, but to no avail.

Oakley must have enjoyed Chapman's panic but, gentleman that he was, he never let on. He just sat up there conveying a message with his demeanour: "Relax, kid, I know exactly where we are and exactly what to do. Enjoy the ride." Little trestles rumbled and flashed under their wheels, and level crossings—fortunately not in use—shot by. Nothing could be seen. Then, as quickly as it had started, they burst through the fog into a clear night. Chapman's glance returned to the engineer. A very small grin crept into the corners of Fred's mouth. He had enjoyed seeing his fireboy sweating bullets, but he never mentioned it to Chapman or to anyone. Chapman says, "It's sixty-two years ago now, Fred—thanks for the ride!"

The trip west from Hanna to Calgary with Jack O'Brien was an experience Chapman will cherish all his life. One night he got the

call: "Train No. 9 on time—03.30—the hoghead is Jack O'Brien."
This was it. As Chapman recalls, "When Jack left town that night,
there would be guys on the streets of Hanna but *I* would be in that
cab with Jack. We'd do this one together!"

Chapman thought he would wet his pants when the conductor
gave two sharp whistles on the communications line to the cab, signalling a "highball," meaning the train was free to leave the station.
Jack looked over at him, gave a curt nod, "whistled off" (two long
blasts on the engine whistle), released the engine brake, and flipped
on the sanders that would blow sand under the wheels to prevent
them from slipping. He eased the throttle open to feel if he had all
the slack and then pulled it full open. Chapman had never been on
an engine when that had been done.

Everyone, including Chapman, was pretty conservative when let-
ting ninety kilograms of superheated steam (two hundred pounds
per square inch) surge into the massive cylinders. Here was snorting-
big power, and things were going to happen. The drivers wanted to
spin as they strained to get traction on the shiny steel. But Jack was
with it all the way. Each time the engine wanted to "lose her feet,"
he inched the reverser ever so little—shortening the valve stroke. It
was a delicate balance keeping maximum power while still control-
ling the tendency to slip. He kept maximum throttle and let her bite
into the sandy rail, throwing cannon fire exhausts at the skies. Now
the exhausts were increasing in intensity. Salvos of sound struck the
grain elevators and smashed back at the engine, and echoes galloped
across town, reverberating through yards and sending windows into
a nervous clatter. There was a brief slowing of the exhausts during
the mandatory brake test (required after leaving the station) that
dragged the speed down.

Then, they were back in earnest. Whack, whack, whack… it
was glorious! Jack was leaving town, and he was taking Chapman
with him. They shot west up the right-of-way, headed for Watts,

Craigmyle, Delia, on to Drumheller, then up the hill through Rockyford to Calgary. Today, Chapman says of his old friend, "That was sixty-two years ago. Sorry I never thanked you for that ride, Jack, a ride I have carried with me ever since."

Chapman's wish is that someone reads this a long time from now and remembers these two fine gentlemen, Fred Oakley and Jack O'Brien—two of the best!

MIRACLE BELOW SAVONA

Former carman Joe Smuin at Canyon Creek Bridge (now known as Pooley Creek Bridge) on Myra Canyon. **KEVIN WITZKE**

JOE SMUIN started his railway career in the CPR's mechanical department at Penticton, BC, in 1974. In 1977, he left CPR to begin a carman's apprenticeship on the British Columbia Railway. He spent most of his career as a carman (inspecting and maintaining rolling stock) in the BC Rail Yard at North Vancouver before retiring in 2004. He is a Kettle Valley Railway historian and has written two books about the KVR.

The year was 1975. The ground shook as the heavily loaded CPR coal train departed on its westbound journey from the CP Rail

Yard office at Kamloops to Roberts Bank, just south of Vancouver. Two powerful diesel-electric locomotives rumbled through the station. Farther back in the long train were three remotely-controlled "slaves" (unmanned locomotives) and a "robot car" that contained the radio receiver and controls for the slaves.

Around midnight, Joe Smuin and his partner had just finished ensuring that the coal train's locomotives were in working order. "As the slaves throbbed by, suspicious activity caught my eye," recalled Joe. "Two men and a woman were on the front platform of one of the units. I thought they must have climbed up just before the train started moving."

The trio awkwardly made their way into the cab of the unit, and Joe could see they were intoxicated. Normally in such situations, employees would get on the radio and stop the train to have police remove unauthorized riders if they didn't think it safe to do it themselves. For some reason, Joe just couldn't be bothered that night, though he realized later that he should have.

Within a few minutes, the train had made its way into the cold, dry wintry night. Things were quiet, but not for long. Just after 1:00 a.m., No. 2, the eastbound passenger train known as The Canadian, radioed the yard office to request that an ambulance be standing by when the train arrived at the Kamloops station. The crew had picked up an injured woman lying on the tracks west of Savona and were bringing her in. An ambulance was duly summoned, and paramedics were ready to lift her down when the train arrived. Joe Smuin watched as she was unloaded from the baggage car into the ambulance.

The crews of the two trains had two amazing stories to tell, though it took a few days for the details to emerge. The crew of the westbound coal train had no idea, of course, that anybody was riding the slave units. The hogger (engineer) on that train estimated that at the point where the woman was found lying between the rails, he had been going around fifty-five kilometres per hour (35 miles).

It seems that at some point, the woman Smuin had spotted on the train had needed to urinate and had gone onto the platform of the engine and squatted, attempting to "go" between the units. She lost her balance and fell—apparently between the two locomotives—and ended up lying on the cross-ties between the rails. At least one locomotive, fifty loaded coal cars, and a caboose managed to pass over her—with a clearance of around twenty-five centimetres (ten inches)—without killing her. It was a miracle that she had fallen in such a way that she wasn't dragged by the locomotive or hit by the rest of the equipment passing over her.

The Canadian was guided by a nervous old engineman that night. He was a bit high-strung and had glittery black eyes that missed nothing. His fireman that night was somewhat younger and less cautious. They came around a curve onto a long tangent when both spotted something between the rails far ahead. The fireman thought it was tumbleweed. The old hogger wasn't sure, and the fireman could see he was getting agitated.

Within a few seconds after spotting the object between the rails, the hogger suddenly "plugged" the air brake, putting the train into full emergency-brake application. The train came to a stop just short of the object, which turned out to be an unconscious woman. The question was, how did she get there? They later discovered she was the woman Smuin had seen boarding the slave in Kamloops an hour earlier. She was unconscious, but incredibly, still all in one piece.

Joe Smuin and the other railroaders were amazed that she had lived through the ordeal. "Had the hogger not acted on that instinct, the woman would not have survived," he said. "If she had not been killed outright by No. 2, she would have died from exposure."

Smuin later learned the woman had not broken any bones, though she had significant internal injuries. Why she wasn't shredded to pieces is a mystery.

A DAY OUT OF
THE ORDINARY

BRUCE HARVEY BRINGS a wealth of railroader history to life, as he lived it front and centre. He was born into a railroader family and, until his retirement in 2000, was a railroader himself. A great storyteller, he writes a blog about his railroad experiences (caboosecoffee.ca). One of his exciting stories goes back to Saturday, May 29, 1982. "Four yard switchers sat outside the CN's Port Mann shops, their smoke drifting gently upward in the warm spring sky. The day was bright, and the job was going to be easy—with just the conductor and me, the engineer," he recalls.

That day, the crew was moving locomotives around from one yard to another within the Greater Vancouver terminal. Their assignment was to take the four yard switchers (small locomotives used to assemble trains) from the engine-service track to Vancouver's main yard, a distance of about thirty-two kilometres (twenty miles). Then they were to pick up four similar units, take them another five kilometres (three miles) to Vancouver's Waterfront Yard, couple them up to four more switchers, and bring all eight back to Port Mann.

Armed with orders from the Burlington Northern (BN) dispatcher in New Westminster/Sapperton that would allow them to proceed from the north end of the Fraser River Bridge to Vancouver, the conductor and Harvey checked their watches against the standard railway clock on the wall behind the operator's desk. After performing inspections and a brake test, they were ready to go.

"The dispatcher said we had the entire railroad to ourselves, as there was no traffic expected for at least three hours—a great day for a train ride," remembers Harvey.

They ambled over the Fraser River Bridge to the sound of the GM diesel thrumming happily and the clanking of old tie plates protesting beneath the wheels and on rails below them. The clean, cool smell of the Fraser River wafted through the open windows as they enjoyed what had to be one of the finest views of the river and the old city of New Westminster.

As the engine was about to roll from the trestle onto the swing span, Harvey reduced the throttle just enough to slow the consist by a few kilometres per hour. This reduced the amount of shock that was transmitted up to the bridge tender's offices high above the middle of the span. The Fraser River Bridge was a shaky old lady, and even the movement of a few small yard locomotives could cause her to quiver noticeably. Once off the metal works of the bridge, the train drifted down past the recently closed BC Penitentiary toward Sapperton and the BN Railroad. Whistle blowing like a trombone, bell ringing, headlights on full, they came into view of the station. Harvey gave a couple of short, sharp blasts on the whistle and the dispatcher waved from the window.

Harvey notched up the throttle as they crossed Braid Street to begin the climb up to Burnaby. Once they entered double track at Burnaby, he throttled down, holding the four-locomotive consist at sixty-four kilometres (forty miles) per hour.

Leaving double track, they began to descend through the steep grade to CN Junction, where they lined the train into CN's Vancouver yard. "There didn't seem to be anybody on duty there, so we secured our incoming locomotives on the shop track and climbed onto the four engines that were ready for us and snaked our way over the Burrard Inlet Line to the Waterfront Yard, where we tied on to four more units sitting in front of the yard office," recalls Harvey.

The yardmaster told them that the general yard coordinator at Port Mann had added to their assignment. They were to pick up more locomotives at Lynn Creek Yard in North Vancouver. This was a major detour that involved going partway back on the BN main line and backing into the two-mile tunnel under Burnaby, crossing Burrard Inlet on the Second Narrows Rail Bridge, and running through the yard to the shop track. In Harvey's mind, "It doesn't sound like such a big deal, but crossing Burrard Inlet can involve serious delays if a deep-sea vessel is in the vicinity. Marine traffic almost always takes precedence over rail traffic."

At the shop track at Lynn Creek, two yard engines waited for them. They were going back to Port Mann with ten locomotives! That had to have been some sort of record.

They were about to leave when the yardmaster brought word that they were also to take a 125-car train of empty open-top cars back to Port Mann. These cars had last contained powdered sulphur.

The Second Narrows Bridge operator said he would take the elevator down to the bridge deck with their orders and clearance. Harvey carefully opened the throttle and the train reluctantly began to follow, the slack already being stretched because the train had been standing on a fairly steep grade.

It's uphill from the yard office to the middle of the tunnel, so Harvey had to make sure he had sufficient power to keep the train moving on the grade. With ten locomotives on the line, the train could break apart if the locomotive wheels slipped on the rails, or if Harvey mishandled the throttle and brake settings. At the middle of the lift span, the bridge operator appeared, handing their train orders and clearance to them. He quickly disappeared into the elevator, closing the door against a cloud of fine yellow sulphur dust that was coming from the empty cars in the train. Automatic sanding circuits kept cutting in whenever the wheels began to slip or spin, dumping small amounts of dry silica sand onto the rails for traction.

Harvey couldn't even temporarily shut off the sanders, because without sand, even for an instant, the locomotives would slip and surge with disastrous results. This would leave them sitting, straddling the Second Narrows, unable to move until repairs were made. With the possibility of large, ocean-going ships approaching, themselves unable to stop, the train had to keep moving at all costs.

As the train moved off the bridge, it immediately entered the three-kilometre (two-mile) tunnel beneath Burnaby. It was to be a long, hard climb up the hill to the middle of the tunnel.

Some of the units had been sitting idle for up to sixteen hours since their last working shift, and as they got hotter and hotter, they released massive amounts of smoke and sparks inside the tunnel.

Within a couple of minutes, blue and red alarm lights blinked on Harvey's control stand, and clanging alarm bells filled the cab with noise, indicating that one or more of the ten locomotives had shut down. With train speed dropping due to the loss of power, Harvey had to make a quick decision: stop inside the tunnel and try to restart the dead units, or proceed out of the tunnel into the fresh air. He decided to continue to the open air and park on the BN main line. He felt that they could solve the problem without blocking that track for too long. Before leaving the tunnel, he looked back to see the most amazing light show: golf-ball-sized chunks of flaming carbon were being thrown from the exhaust stacks! They were going straight up, hitting the ceiling of the tunnel, and dropping into the empty hopper cars behind the engine. (Hopper cars carry bulk material like sulphur or other commodities that can be discharged through the floor through manually operated doors.)

With the train rolling slowly ahead, the utility man went back through the ten-unit consist to restart the three units that had shut down. A couple of them could not be restarted, so he left them dead in the consist.

They continued toward the Fraser River Rail Bridge, but not without trepidation. If another locomotive in the consist failed while on the bridge, they could be in deep trouble, as marine traffic would have to wrestle with their heavily loaded barges to avoid a collision with the bridge span. The conductor reminded Harvey that if they couldn't make the bridge, they would have crossings blocked on the BN main line as well. Harvey called the BN dispatcher and the bridge to tell them of their predicament. The dispatcher said he would have the signals set for them if they decided to go for it. The bridge operator said that the bridge was currently lined for them, but if a tug called, he'd have to open the bridge and hold back the train. Harvey gambled. He opened the throttle to take a run at the bridge. He advised the operator that they would be approaching at a pretty rapid rate, but the length of the train would slow them down to something that might resemble a "reasonable" speed for the crossing of the span.

They entered the bridge interlocking (an arrangement of interconnected signals, turnouts, and routings that three major railroads and all marine traffic had to share) at more than sixteen kilometres (ten miles) per hour—twice the legal limit—and only just managed to keep the train moving as it climbed up the 1 percent grade to the bridge. The engines roared and bucked under the strain as they clawed their way over the swing span. Their speed dropped to a crawl, but as more of the train pulled up onto the level span, they were soon back at eight kilometres (five miles) per hour.

That's when Harvey realized that all those golf-ball-sized chunks of burning carbon had been landing in the empty sulphur cars, but that the cars weren't exactly empty. The contents had been unloaded in North Vancouver after a long trip from Alberta, but some powdered sulphur had stuck to the inside of each car. When they'd hauled the train out of the yard, the sulphur had dropped into the bottoms of the cars and gathered in the hoppers there. And that's where the burning carbon went, too.

The burning sulphur had turned into a molten mess and was dripping from the cars onto the railway roadbed, creosoted ties, and the bridge timbers. It was then that both the bridge operator and the dispatcher called them with alarm in their voices. Harvey remembers it vividly: "The damned train was on fire!"

The bridge operator immediately ordered Harvey to get off the bridge as quickly as possible. The operator's office was an ancient wooden structure perched high above the swing span in the middle of the bridge. While the operator couldn't see any flames forming on the bridge, he reasonably assumed there soon would be. In order to avert a major fire, he alerted firefighting forces. A train of 125 cars is about two kilometres (a mile and a quarter) long. It wasn't going to get across the full length of the span and the timbered approaches anytime soon, even if Harvey increased the speed dramatically.

Harvey had to first make sure that he didn't do anything that would cause the train to derail. Second, he had to notify all concerned about their situation to ensure there were no trains blocking their way once they got off the bridge and its approaches.

Harvey changed radio channels and contacted the yardmaster at Port Mann. With their train on fire, they couldn't risk stopping anywhere between the bridge and a secure track in the yard. There were several industries along that stretch of track, including lumber mills, manufacturers, and fuel suppliers. "I asked him to ensure that all movements in and around the west end of the yard were well clear of our route into the yard and to line our train into a track that could easily be serviced by the Surrey Fire Department," recalls Harvey.

The approach to the bridge and portions of the bridge deck were now on fire, and the train was again ordered to get off the bridge so that fire crews could respond.

CN engineer Bruce Harvey in Oyama, BC, on his last shift and on his way to Vernon, BC—and retirement, on January 6, 2000. **D. BROOKE RUSKIN, FORMER PRESIDENT OF THE OKANAGAN VALLEY RAILWAY**

The on-duty utility man at Port Mann managed to get all the switches lined up for them, and with a low throttle, the burning train pulled into the yard. As the head end of their train began to enter track 103, Harvey noticed something rather disconcerting. The two tracks on either side of them—102 and 104—held two trains, each containing many cars of dangerous commodities.

Harvey had no idea that the bridge was on fire, but flames had broken out immediately after the train had passed over the span.

A small shed used to store drums of lubricating oil was soon ablaze, and the fire had very quickly climbed upward to engulf the bridge control tower.

Drums of stove oil, used for the control tower's heating system, exploded, sending a huge fireball high above the traffic deck of the nearby Pattullo Bridge, where a crowd had gathered to watch the Fraser River Rail Bridge burn.

The Fraser River Rail Bridge operator barely escaped with his life as the tower became completely engulfed in flames. Firefighters from both New Westminster and Surrey, the two communities connected by the Fraser River Rail Bridge and the Pattullo vehicle-traffic bridge, attended the scene. Several tugboats also pumped water onto the burning structure from below.

Meanwhile, Harvey quietly finished his shift and went home. In the excitement generated by the spectacular fire on the rail bridge, the arrival of Harvey's smouldering train of dripping, molten sulphur residue was soon forgotten where it stopped in the rail yard.

The rail tracks on the Fraser River Rail Bridge suffered serious damage caused by the fire that Harvey's burning sulphur train caused on that beautiful day in May 1982. That rail crossing of the Fraser River was closed to traffic for weeks while trains were detoured via other routes.

WHICH PIECE GOES WHERE?

BRAD COATES IS a locomotive engineer who had a vision to rescue and restore a decrepit ninety-year-old steam locomotive and bring it back to life where he worked at the Kettle Valley Steam Railway in Summerland, BC.

Locomotive No. 3716 is a charming steam locomotive with an enviable reputation. Best known for its starring role in several movies, it was the proud backup to the Royal Hudson locomotive on its scenic BC Rail run between North Vancouver and Squamish, BC, from 1978 to 2001.

When BC Rail retired the locomotive, the provincial government issued a tender for its long-term lease, and Coates leapt at the opportunity. Why not bring it to Summerland to replace the Kettle Valley Steam Railway's Shay locomotive, which was on loan from the BC Forest Discovery Centre?

But the government wasn't about to lease the locomotive to just anyone. They wanted assurance that it would be maintained and operated. How could Coates assure the government that his idea was feasible, given some major obstacles?

For example, without a railway from North Vancouver to Summerland, in BC's Interior, the only way to transport the huge machine was by truck for nearly 400 kilometres (250 miles), and the logistics presented a formidable challenge. Few companies in BC and Alberta would be able to do the job. So Coates turned to Ed Kinvig, an expert in moving heavy equipment whose work on size, weight,

Brad Coates in Locomotive No. 3716's smokebox (the front part of the boiler on which the smokestack sits). **BRAD COATES**

dimensions, routes, cranes, and myriad Transport Canada regulations contributed to winning the bureaucrats over. The project was deemed a "go." (*Continued on page 129.*)

A NATIONAL ICON COMES ABOARD

FROM HIS PERCH in the cab, engineer Ron Restrick revelled in the belches, hisses, and pops from steam locomotive No. 3716—ah, yes, it was like music to his ears.

Beside him, the fireman expertly tweaked the fine, ninety-two-year-old workhorse into readiness for the scenic ninety-minute journey that began in North Vancouver and snaked its way along Howe Sound to Squamish.

From the nearby platform, a group of tourists eagerly waited to board the Royal Hudson train for its 10:30 a.m. departure.

Restrick threw an empty coffee cup into the firebox and tucked it away out of sight. It simply wouldn't be acceptable to have the cab look anything but tidy, especially today. Fortunately, the rain clouds had lifted earlier, giving way to the clear skies of a warm June morning: perfect conditions in which to welcome a very special guest.

"Good morning," quavered a white-haired man standing near the track. "I may need a hand climbing up this long ladder."

Restrick instantly recognized the familiar voice, even with its flagging intensity. Jumping down from the cab to help, he noted the famous Canadian's style trademark, a bow tie.

"Good morning, Mr. Berton. Glad to have you aboard!"

Restrick was beyond thrilled. Here, in his cab, amid the chuffing and snorting, was an icon of Canadian literature, the marvellous storyteller and esteemed journalist Pierre Berton.

Restrick's eyes misted over. He felt humbled. "Mr. Berton, I want to tell you how enthralled I was reading your historical novel about Louis Riel," he began.

Pierre Berton during the filming of the TV series *The Last Spike*, based on his book of the same name. Berton also wrote *The National Dream: The Great Railway, 1871–1881.* CANADIAN PACIFIC RAILWAY

Pierre Berton listened patiently to Restrick's praise for the book. "Well, yes, it is a fine book," he agreed politely. "But I didn't write it."

The fireman snickered at the faux pas, and the embarrassed Restrick winced at his mistake.

Berton manoeuvred his way into the engineer's seat, his boyish grin revealing intense delight. He poked his head out of the window as an engineer would—looking back along the track and then forward.

"Go ahead," encouraged Restrick. "Give the steam whistle a couple of toots."

Despite his frailness and the considerable tension on the whistle, Berton pulled hard. There it was—that unmistakable, haunting sound that so charmingly evoked bygone eras.

The moment was fleeting. Berton was too frail to stay on board longer, and riding in the cab to Squamish would have been too uncomfortable.

Restrick and the fireman helped him down, and the much-loved Canadian waved a wistful goodbye.

Over twelve days in March 2003, Coates and seven volunteers painstakingly dismantled No. 3716. Six flatbed trucks lined up in the rail yard: one each for the boiler, frame (running gear), cab, tender tank, tender frame, driving rods, and loose parts.

"Some loads were easy, but the boiler, weighing 45,350 kilograms (100,000 pounds) and the running gear, weighing between that and 54,430 kilograms (100,000 to 120,000 pounds) were more difficult. We had to travel at night because we were hauling heavy, dangerous loads," recalled Coates.

At 10:00 p.m. on March 11, the trucks pulled out of the rail yard. Truckers and Transport Canada were in communication regarding which route to take to Summerland, with load, height, and other restrictions playing an important role. Three loads went via the Coquihalla Highway, while the others went via Highway 3. "We had problems with weight," said Coates. "We couldn't go over the Port Mann Bridge because of restrictions, and at one weigh station in the Fraser Valley, we were within forty-five kilograms [a hundred pounds] of not being allowed to proceed."

It was slow going. The trucks couldn't exceed eighty kilometres (fifty miles) per hour, had to stop frequently to check loads, and even had to go around one bridge on the Coquihalla Highway. They arrived in Summerland at seven the next morning, marshalling in the yards of the former West Summerland Train Station.

Cranes lifted the running gear onto the rails first, placed the boiler on top, then the cab. When the parts were all put together, the Shay pulled No. 3716 the five kilometres (three miles) to the shop at the KVR Steam Railway.

"What have I got myself into?" wondered Coates (who is also a boilermaker and locomotive mechanic) as he and three volunteers began the eighteen-month-long project to restore No. 3716. The boiler needed the most work. It required a new firebox, new tubes, and a smokebox.

"But the whole engine needed a refurbishment, and because we had to take the boiler apart... [W]hile you're in that deep, you might as well go through everything with a fine-tooth comb.

"There was a surprise every day!" laughed Coates. "Some days I felt I got a lot done; but there were also dark days." Fortunately, long-time master mechanic/millwright George Williamson and boiler-maker Beatty Davis from the BC Forest Discovery Centre arrived to share their experience and knowledge.

"The firebox (where fuel is burned and consumed) had to be removed because plate metal had deteriorated. It was a major job. I remember looking up and thinking, holy smokes—how am I ever going to get this back together? I felt lost," said Coates.

"That job was daunting and very complex. The firebox is part of the boiler, so you have to follow the engineering [i.e., go by the original blueprints and drawings used to build the engine]. You can't just wing it. It's designed a certain way, so if you step out of the engineering, you're going to have failure. You have to stick to a plan. Some parts were really worn out."

If Coates's team needed new parts, they had to make them. "We received a set of boiler-design drawings from the National Museum in Ottawa. I was able to follow the original design. But then we discovered that the CPR had made alterations to the design several times. So we had to discover what alterations, if any, were made on this engine."

Thousands of pieces of No. 3716 required refurbishing and reassembly. The tasks seemed endless: dismantle the running gear, replace bearings, clean steel and steam piping, rebuild the injector, the water pump, air pump, and generator—the list went on and on. But it was that darned boiler that continued to cause Coates stress.

"The boiler is a pressure vessel made of steel, and with time, steel curls and erodes," explained Brad. "When it becomes thin, it gets weak and won't hold as much pressure. So in a boiler, you want to make sure every piece of steel will not fail. There are lots of pieces that need to be checked frequently to ensure failures won't happen. Unfortunately, there are parts that are unseen unless you dismantle it. I didn't know who had worked on it previously; there were few inspections, no record on history of parts and pieces. So we had to go through everything.

"The boiler can be a bomb if not operated properly. It holds ninety kilograms [two hundred pounds] of steam pressure, and it's different from air pressure. Steam has an expansive force. One drop of boiling water expands 1,600 times its original size. If I'm in charge of a dangerous piece of equipment I'm going to ensure no one gets hurt because of ignorance or negligence."

Finally, in spring 2005, the grand old locomotive was ready to strut its stuff; it did not disappoint. "It was a good day, but one of the most stressful days of my life," recalled Coates. "I threw the rag in the firebox, lit the fire, brought the boiler pressure up, and did a couple of test runs. Everything worked!"

Nine years later, Coates still pours the same amount of passion into No. 3716's well-being. It's in his blood, and he knows many more passengers will yet thrill at the quaint chuff-chuff and clouds of steam as it pulls away from the KVR station.

CANADIAN PACIFIC RAILWAY'S Kettle Valley Division saw many 2-8-0s not unlike No. 3716. No. 3716 was built as a coal-burning locomotive in 1912 by Montreal Locomotive Works. It was named No. 3916, was rebuilt in 1929, and rechristened No. 3716.

Its home for many years was in the Kootenays, and No. 3716 ran many kilometres in the Crowsnest area of southern British Columbia and Alberta. Later in its career, it was converted from coal to oil. Having been saved by the scrapper's torch, No. 3716 went to the City of Port Coquitlam in 1966.

No. 3716 was restored to operating condition by 1975 at CPR's Drake Street shops. It was put to work on the Provincial Museum train touring the province and made a trip on the Kettle Valley line in 1977, including Summerland and the Osoyoos branch of the KVR.

No. 3716 starred in many movies and commercials over the years, including *The Grey Fox,* a movie about Billy Miner, and *The Journey of Natty Gann*, a Walt Disney Production. No. 3716 ran charters into the Cariboo and worked as a backup to the Royal Hudson (No. 2860) until its operating career on BC Rail ended in April 2001.

Steam-train trips enthral visitors to historic Big Valley near Stettler, Alberta.
ALBERTA PRAIRIE RAILWAY PHOTO

TRACKSIDE BEDTIME STORIES

THESE ARE STORIES you could mesmerize your listeners with. A legendary, mild-mannered outlaw named Bill Miner has a talent for prison escapes that surpasses even his predilection for robbing trains. A train is swallowed up in broad daylight by the boggy ground near Burnaby Lake. And a railroad employee recalls the mystery that shrouded a certain train trip whose mission was top secret.

◄ The CPR 2024 steam engine features prominently during Railway Days at Calgary Heritage Park. **CALGARY HERITAGE PARK**

BILLY MINER'S
MISSING LOOT

"HANDS UP!" The words, spoken in a drawl, startled the train engineer on the CPR's Transcontinental No. 1 as it steamed westward near Mission Junction. It was an opening line that notorious stagecoach robber William Miner had created forty years earlier and continued to use as he robbed coaches in such states as California, New Mexico, and Colorado. W.M. Pinkerton of the Pinkerton Detective Agency had declared Billy Miner "the master criminal of the American West."

This latest heist came as the Transcontinental reached Silverdale, about sixty-five kilometres (forty miles) east of Vancouver, on Saturday, September 10, 1904. What alarmed Engineer N.J. Scott even more than Billy Miner's command were the two revolvers Miner was pointing at him and his coal-shovelling fireman, Harry Freeman—and also the rifle held by the cocky Shorty Dunn, who was standing next to a third intruder, Louis Colquhoun, looking every bit the dishevelled burglar and who was also levelling two more revolvers their way. A misty autumn fog enveloped the cab, shrouding the three men with an air of mystery. But their masked faces made their intentions clear.

It was 9:30 p.m. The Transcontinental (also known as the Express) was two and a half hours behind schedule and about to be delayed a little longer while it gained notoriety as Canada's best-known train robbery.

The fifty-eight-year-old Miner, five foot nine and the thinnest of the three, might have earned the nickname "Shorty" if Dunn were not beside him. What set him apart were his polite manners and a voice frequently recalled as having a gentleman's tone. In that relaxed voice, he told Scott, "I want you to stop the train at the Silverdale crossing." As the engineer complied, the passengers aboard the two coaches following behind had little reason to imagine anything untoward; trains slowed or stopped frequently to let others pass or to put distance between one train and another for reasons of safety. Within a short while, the locomotive shuddered and came to rest eight kilometres (five miles) west of Mission, as directed. Miner said, "Do what you are told and not a hair of your head will be harmed."

The consist began with three important components: the engine, the coal tender, and the express car (used to contain items such as mail, merchandise, or currency, and a safe). Harry Freeman was led to the rear of the express car and told to uncouple it from the rest of the train. It was a jarring and cumbersome process that jolted the cars left behind as the engine pulled away.

The disruption sparked concerns and confusion onboard. Several travellers relaxed, while others talked with fellow passengers anxious to get to Vancouver. A gunshot rang out. A panicked porter raced through the coaches saying the engineer was dead and that a robbery was under way. Men and women hid jewellery and stuffed money into cushions and seatbacks, having read news stories of brutality and theft on American trains as robbers ruthlessly collected valuables from passengers.

Back in the engine's cab, Miner told a very-much-alive engineer Scott and Freeman to "Go to Whonnock Mile Post and stop in front of the wharf." Minutes later, when the three-part train halted in the quiet setting, Miner and an accomplice stepped down and walked to the door of the Express coach, where Miner threatened the manager of the express car, Herbert Mitchell, saying, "Open up, or we'll blow the door down with dynamite." Mitchell took out his .38 Smith & Wesson but thought better and tucked it into his clothes. He opened the door. When Mitchell jumped down from the coach, Miner frisked him, found the hidden gun, and took it for his own, saying, "Now open up that safe."

Express cars often proved a treasure trove of gold dust, bonds, and banknotes that were either destined for places such as the Bank of British North America or for payrolls. Registered mail often contained money tucked neatly within a parcel sent from one family member to another or between commercial enterprises. As Mitchell fiddled with the safe, Miner strolled around casually yet determinedly throughout the coach, retrieving packages that interested him by their heft or address. One contained $50,000 (easily worth over $1 million today) of railway bonds—bonds that to this day have neither been cashed nor found; these remain at the heart of the legend surrounding "Billy Miner's missing loot," over a century later.

Miner was disappointed when the safe door was finally opened: missing was the $62,000 gold shipment he had been anticipating. He had learned the Consolidated Cariboo Mine was transferring gold from Ashcroft to Vancouver, so this expectation had motivated their selection of this particular train. That gold had missed a connection and was not on board. Nonetheless, their take for half an hour was substantial.

As the gang of three took their leave, Billy Miner, in a genteel drawl, admonished the engineer to be careful backing down the track without proper lighting. He left them with a thoughtful "Goodnight, boys!"

As slick as that, Western Canada's first train robbery was over, the occurrence so novel that only once before (on November, 13, 1874, Great Western Railway evening express out of Hamilton bound for Toronto) had a train in Canada been accosted. As the Billy Miner gang left the Transcontinental, its passengers were safe, the crew unharmed, and many good rumours begun.

The BC Provincial Police and the CPR's police immediately pursued Miner and his gang. The Dominion Express Company posted a reward. In a nod to US experience in tracking thieves who targeted trains, an invitation was extended to the Pinkerton Detective Agency to help. Cross-border crime escapades were not infrequent, and a recent incident involving robbers of the Oregon Railroad and Navigation Company occurred under circumstances similar to the CPR heist. Might they be connected? They were, in the mind of Pinkerton's superintendent James Dye, who joined the pursuit.

It is thought that Miner, as leader of the gang, held on to the bulk of the stolen loot after divvying up part of their bounty for his partners. They then split up in different directions. Having anticipated the $62,000 gold delivery, it is reasonable to presume Miner had a nearby hiding site chosen in order to rid himself of any evidence while the proximity of their whereabouts was known. A prevailing theory is that Miner, without his accomplices knowing, hid that cache of $50,000 in bonds at his secret place near Whonnock, or Silverdale, maybe even closer to Mission Junction. Then he fled the area. Miner's future spending habits never revealed such wealth. Many believe the money still lies stashed and buried, waiting to be found.

With the Canada-US border only nineteen kilometres (twelve miles) from the Whonnock robbery site, hunts for the men took place near and around the crossing. Authorities suspected the men would flee south, Miner being an American. Posses fanned out around Sumas Lake, along the banks of the Fraser River, and near Lynden in Washington State. When the fruitless search was abandoned in the ensuing weeks, Pinkerton's James Dye held on to his belief that he knew who the perpetrator was, saying afterward that

"Bill Miner was the mastermind behind the Portland train robbery and the holdup at Mission Junction."

Billy Miner hailed from Kentucky, where he'd been born in the late 1840s. His fixed address, however, was often San Quentin State Prison, where he had four extended visits. Over his career, he also met cellmates in other locations such as the BC Penitentiary in New Westminster and a Georgia prison. His more traditional work life was erratic and included stints as cowpoke, lumber-mill worker, Pony Express rider, electrician, farmer, and rancher. Most often, though, he robbed Wells Fargo stagecoaches, and twice stole from a coach operated by Del Norte in Colorado. As stagecoaches were being replaced by railway services, Miner adapted to the times. When he was successful, the stolen funds enabled his deportment to be that of a handsome gentleman. Those who met him remember a gregarious man fitted out for leisure time in one town with financial resources from elsewhere. Miner used many aliases, one of which was George Edwards, under which he lived comfortably as a welcomed resident in Princeton, BC, for the two years after his robbery of the Transcontinental Express. Yet nothing about his behaviour indicated a man with ready access to $50,000.

Either to replenish his money, or for the excitement of the experience, Billy Miner eventually returned to his robbery routine, always with the reassuring presence that defined his style. Enhanced by his firm-brimmed or floppy hats, great coats, and greying hair, a notably grand moustache and a calm drone, his "Hands up!" greeting became a trademark. He was arrested and jailed almost as frequently as he robbed. Just as assuredly, he regularly escaped prison, hiding away until his next heist or until he was caught. Inevitably, he began the pattern all over again: robbery, arrest, escape, hiding. Whenever he was on the loose, he most often resided within a community as a respected citizen.

Did he leave his hidden stash near Whonnock as a rainy-day reserve? Or was he unable to get back to it? If so, where is it today?

Billy Miner's heist of another CPR passenger train two years after the Silverdale robbery, on May 8, 1906, was less successful. A three-member gang struck the Imperial Limited as it throttled toward Kamloops on its westbound course to Vancouver. At what is today Monte Creek but was then called Ducks, Miner and two associates boarded the train, crawled across the coal tender, and surprised the engineer and fireman with his command, "Hands up!" Having soon separated the engine and coal tender along with the third car and moved them a safe distance down the track from the rest of the train, they prepared to open the safe. Then alarm struck: "This isn't the express car. It's the baggage car!" shouted one of the gang. They had mistakenly decoupled the mail car. Despite the disappointing take ($15 from two envelopes), when they left the train crew, Miner offered his usual, "Goodnight, boys. Take care of yourselves."

Sought by the North-West Mounted Police and the BC Provincial Police, and with renewed cooperation from Pinkerton, the thieves were traced most effectively by Constable William Fernie. It was due to the skills of five Native trackers that the robbers' trail was followed, over a week-long pursuit, through Douglas Lake country to an old cabin, where they posed as prospectors. Using the alias George Edwards, Miner chuckled to the police, "We do not look much like train robbers," but the three were apprehended and put on trial in Kamloops.

Public sympathy during the hearing was with the accused. The first trial, despite its detailed prosecution, delivered an inconclusive verdict to the courtroom. This necessitated a second trial, by which time the celebrity status of Billy Miner was palpable on the streets. Miner was not flattered by the police description of his lengthy life of crime, yet he was proud of their observation that "he claims to be

In spring 1906, the gentleman train robber Billy Miner, later known as "the Grey Fox," was arrested and put on trial in Kamloops. He appeared relaxed when photographer Mary Spencer caught this pose on behalf of Vancouver's *Province* newspaper. IMAGE A-01617 ROYAL BC MUSEUM AND ARCHIVES

sixty-two, looks like a man of fifty, and moves like one of thirty." In many towns along North American railways in those days, there was cynicism about railway companies and their focus on profit and demeaning approach to employees. The public's sympathy was clear: "Billy Miner's not so bad. He only robs the CPR once every two years, but the CPR robs us all every day."

On June 1, 1906, the three robbers were convicted and sentenced to life in prison for their robbery of $15, the sentence reflecting the severity of the crime, not the amount taken. The convicts were transferred to the BC Penitentiary. A year later, in August, Billy Miner escaped, leaving behind his treasured gold pocket watch.

Accusations swirled in newspapers and Parliament that Miner had been aided in his prison escape by the federal government as part of their deal to find the missing $50,000 taken from the Transcontinental Express near Silverdale.

Two years after this escape, as Miner remained at large, accusations of deal making and political payoffs reached the highest office of the land, forcing Canada's prime minister, Sir Wilfrid Laurier, to deny the involvement of his government. Laurier told the House of Commons, "The question which interests this country is whether there has been any connivance on the part of anybody in the escape of Bill Miner. No more dangerous criminal, I think, was ever in the clutches of Canadian justice."

Billy Miner was in Pennsylvania, where news from Canada was infrequent, and he'd have been unaware of the turmoil. Living under the name George Anderson, a sawmill employee, he was a reliable worker and respected fellow in the eyes of all who knew him. Alas, temptation was only a whistle away, as he lived within earshot of passing trains. Even as he aged, he could not resist the lure of one last, uninvited visit to an express coach. His ability to find able accomplices for a high-stakes train robbery was still intact. He ventured to Virginia with a new partner in tow, and there they added another to make up his preferred complement of three. The ever-courteous Billy Miner led his gang to rob the New York Southern Express near Gainesville, Georgia.

Apprehended and tried, he was convicted on March 11, 1911. Miner faced extradition to Canada to complete his sentence at the BC Penitentiary. The state of Georgia, confident of its secure prison setup, wanted to keep the sixty-five-year-old, and they did. They felt the senior citizen was weak and worn and posed no threat whatsoever.

On October 21 of that year, Miner escaped prison. Soon cornered in a boxcar after using a route through a swamp that nearly killed him, Miner was returned to Georgia's prison "to serve out a twenty-year sentence for robbing a Southern Railway train."

Eight months later, on June 29, 1912, a thunderstorm struck in the prison's community. An ever-prepared sixty-six-year-old Billy Miner took full advantage of the disruption and once again escaped prison. Found, captured, and returned, the fever-ridden Miner died on September 2, 1913, making what a newspaper article termed his "third escape from the Georgia penitentiary."

The legendary train robber's passing was news in many states and across both the countries where he'd plied his trade, faced jurisprudence, and served time—and continually escaped incarceration. What keeps the Billy Miner story alive today are not just the books about his escapades, the 1980s film depicting his avuncular approach as "the Grey Fox," or the mountain near Princeton renamed Mount Miner in his honour. It is not even that his gold pocket watch, which he left behind in his 1907 escape from prison, is on display at Victoria's Royal BC Museum.

What keeps the lore of Billy Miner vivid is that the missing funds from his 1904 robbery of the CPR's Transcontinental Express No. 1 have never been found. It may just be a matter of time. Residential development near Whonnock and Silverdale has levelled forests, dug up dirt, and moved boulders. Hikers increasingly frequent old trails and haunts near the railway tracks. Treasure seekers and historians await the day some lucky sod poking about shouts, "Look at what I've found!" In all the excitement, you can bet they'll throw their hands up.

SUNKEN ENGINE CREEK

A LUSH VALLEY cuts across the centre of BC's Metro Vancouver region. Today, it is home to two beautiful lakes, a verdant woodland with a revitalized creek, a freeway, railroad tracks, and burgeoning industry in suburban Burnaby—and a venerable rail legend.

The shallow waters of Burnaby Lake are a sparkling centrepiece in this urban landscape. But just a few metres in any direction, the pace of modern life nudges against its quiet.

To the north of the lake, clusters of small industrial malls have risen just a stone's throw from the peaty ground that borders the lake's shore. The slow-moving waters of Still Creek empty into Burnaby Lake at its western marshes, and the Brunette River flows out the east end, carrying water down through sometimes chaotic descents to the Fraser River.

Two sets of rails on the north side of Burnaby Lake carry a daily variety of trains that rumble through. For many decades, the tracks belonged to Burlington Northern Santa Fe (BNSF), the descendant of Great Northern, which originally laid them, but more recently, CN purchased that route from BNSF. Today, thundering freights and sleek passenger consists from BNSF, CP, CN, VIA, Amtrak, and the Rocky Mountaineer, all of which move on the line, interrupt the silence surrounding the lake from time to time. It is these tracks that cover a mystery that goes back a century, to the early days when peat bogs surrounded the lake and extended for kilometres in either direction.

The land around the lake epitomizes the word "bog." Centuries of peat growth have sucked the waters of the valley into the land and made it deep and fertile. Still Creek winds along just south of the tracks here, and while it was once relegated to being a sewer, today the creek boasts new life in its waters because efforts to clean it up and revitalize it have been remarkably successful. But while the interweaving of roots and decomposing greenery and urban waterways make for lush surroundings, it does not make for good, solid foundations for railroad tracks. And so it was that one locomotive may have come to an ignominious end here.

The east-west valley in Burnaby was largely undeveloped until the middle of the twentieth century. The railroad had been put through that territory about fifty years earlier, but little other human activity had occurred. A few farms, the odd homestead, a bedraggled road here and there—these were the only signs of habitation in this sodden land.

In 1962, the Trans-Canada Highway (Highway 1) was routed through this valley. The builders of the section through Burnaby faced one significant challenge after another as they laid the roadbed atop the peat base of the valley. In places, the land was so soft that repeated dumps of layers of sawdust, mulch, gravel, and even piles were required to support the overpasses and roadbeds associated with a major metropolitan freeway.

And so it was with the railroad that wound its way along the north side of Burnaby Lake many decades earlier. The young port of Vancouver was growing rapidly on the shores of Burrard Inlet, just a few kilometres to the west, and the Great Northern pushed its tracks from Seattle to the south through the Lower Mainland, once the Fraser River had been bridged in the early years of the twentieth century. Traffic along this route became a daily routine.

Then one day, according to local legend, the railbed simply disappeared. A sinkhole opened up, and the tracks slipped beneath exposed groundwater. All service was halted, and crews rushed to the scene to deal with the crisis. Day after day, carload after carload of gravel was poured into the hole to rebuild footings for the track.

A company named Grant Smith Construction was reported to have been involved in this track restoration work, and that day, when its hapless employees took a lunch break, they little expected what would happen next. When they returned from their time out, the track, and their locomotive, had disappeared. In a 1959 interview, a man named Nap Peltier, a crew member of the fated train, recounted the tale. He claimed the crew left the train full of gravel sitting on the track, only to find it sunken into the bog upon their return. "All we saw were the tracks going down into the muddy water, with bubbles coming up," he said.

Crews set to work to recover the missing locomotive, and perhaps some of its consist, but to no avail. If the story is true, and there's a certain amount of evidence that it is, the locomotive still sits there today.

What kind of a locomotive is it? No one is certain. A locomotive used by the Grant Smith Construction Company has sat in front of the Creston Museum for many years. Built in 1910, it is a 0-4-0T built by Vulcan Iron Works; the T stands for "tank." Tank locomotives carried their water in a tank that typically straddled the top of the locomotive, thus not requiring a tender. One reference identifies the locomotive in the Burnaby sinking as a 0-4-0T, and because the same company was involved, it's possible this is true. Thus, it would be a small work engine, used for moving supplies back and forth, shunting cars in yards, etc.

Some dismiss the story as an urban legend. Various references to newspaper articles from the day are difficult to confirm because the actual date of the occurrence is unknown. Perhaps the doubt originates with the confusing mix of dates and locations for the tale. Different sources cite the incident as occurring in 1906, 1910, or 1912. Some say it occurred on the north shore of Burnaby Lake, while others cite a location farther west. So is it really an urban legend, or just a story rooted in poorly reported local history? Opinion, as in all such cases, is divided, though sinkholes do occur in many places.

Today, Beecher Creek runs under the Lougheed Highway on the north edge of the valley, alongside some industrial parking lots and then under the tracks, entering Still Creek about three kilometres (two miles) west of Burnaby Lake. Just up from the point where Beecher Creek meets Still Creek is yet another small tributary, this one named Sunken Engine Creek, according to an official map of Burnaby's waterways. Could this name lend credence to the rumoured disappearing train?

The circumstantial evidence of the Grant Smith Company operating the same engine type, the 1959 Peltier interview, and the name Sunken Engine Creek would all seem to corroborate the tale. In the meantime, the mystery remains unsolved.

A ROYAL LOCOMOTIVE
RIDES THE RAILS

THE SIGHT OF the legendary No. 2860 Royal Hudson steam loco-motive on static display at the West Coast Railway Heritage Park in Squamish, BC, leaves many a viewer awestruck. To see it speed-ing past is a singular thrill that has brought many fans to trackside, often armed with cameras, to enjoy the rush of steam power at its finest.

Its immense potential power is obvious from the moment you see this locomotive. At rest, its silent cylinders, unmoving drive shafts, drive wheels around two metres (eighty inches) in circumfer-ence, and its sleek, streamlined profile all point to its ability to cut through the wind at great speed. To see it whiz past under full power, with a blast of its whistle and plumes of exhaust rising from its stack, stirs the passions of onlookers.

The mighty heart of a steam locomotive never "springs" to life. Rather, a simple fire burning wood, coal, or oil grows ever larger, heating water to the point of boiling and beyond. The resulting steam pushes the pistons in the cylinders, which push the main rods, which push the wheels that push the engine along the tracks. The process of getting there takes patience and time—at least several hours to build up a head of steam powerful enough to move driving wheels taller than most people.

The heart of the Royal Hudson beats strongly when the fires ignite, but many times in its life, that heart has lain cold, still, and silent, almost forgotten, a mere reminder of its former glory as it and the other locomotives of its class would tear across the country, bringing rich and poor, and even royalty, to new adventures at the end of the line.

The locomotive in Squamish has the number 2860 emblazoned on its sides and across the back of its tender. First running in 1940, it was the latest in a long line of top locomotives designed to deliver passengers across Canada swiftly and reliably. This class of locomotives had only recently received the "Royal" designation after the stellar performance of the one—No. 2850—that carried King George VI and his wife, Queen Elizabeth, across the country, from east to west, in 1939. It had been unprecedented for one engine to accomplish such a feat, but No. 2850 had done it, and in recognition of this, King George VI had assented to naming the class "the Royal Hudsons." When No. 2860, built by Montreal Locomotive Works, rolled into service the following year, it featured a streamlined shape and royal crowns on the front running boards. This class of locomotive was the first and last to be given royal status outside the UK.

Hudson locomotives have a 4-6-4 wheel arrangement, which was first used by the New York Central Railroad. The class took its name from the Hudson River, along which some NYC lines travelled. There are four wheels on the "leading engine truck" at the front of the engine, six driving wheels, and another four on the trailing truck, located under the firebox and cab. For transporting passengers, this arrangement is ideal. The size of the firebox, where oil is burned to heat water and create the steam that drives the wheels, is much larger than on earlier models, and the four wheels on the trailing truck located behind the driving wheels manage this weight, but the gain is in engine power: when running at full power, the Hudson is an exceptional high-speed locomotive, perfect for crack passenger trains. The nearly two-metre (eighty-inch) driving wheels gave the Royal Hudson a top speed of over 140 kilometres (87 miles) per hour.

The No. 2860 Royal Hudson locomotive sits in its permanent home, the roundhouse in the West Coast Railway Heritage Park in Squamish, BC. **BRIAN ANTONSON**

No. 2860 plied tracks across Western Canada for many years, much of its time spent leading passenger trains between Vancouver and Revelstoke on the Canadian Pacific Railway (CPR). The steam era came to an end for CPR in 1960, and most Hudson engines were relegated to the scrap heap as the more efficient, less expensive, easier-to-run diesel engines took over their duties.

Only a few survived the cull. No. 2860 was thought to be gone, but then some enthusiasts found it sitting on a track in Vancouver, not yet reduced to scrap, and the idea was born to refurbish it and put it on display. For several years, it sat in the CPR roundhouse in False Creek, its tender sticking out through the back doors, as the locomotive and tender were too long to fit inside. Enthusiasts would pay visits to admire the huge black beauty sitting quietly in forced retirement.

In 1972, a new government was elected in BC, and one of the dreams of the new premier, Dave Barrett, was to launch a tourist train running up and down the stunning shores of Howe Sound, between North Vancouver and Squamish, a route where sea, sky, mountain, and meadow come together and stunning natural panoramas are around every curve.

If ever a location was meant for a tourist train, this was it, and since the railway was owned by the provincial government, the die was cast. Famed diesel locomotive train-horn manufacturer Robert Swanson took the lead on restoring the locomotive, and in 1974, No. 2860 returned to steam, and it led a consist of passenger cars up and down Howe Sound. Passengers flocked to the romance of the rails, enjoying the passing scenery and climbing into the cab for a look-see at either end of the trip. The clarion call of No. 2860's whistle echoed from shore to shore on the Sound, and avid onlookers stood rail side, snapping photos as it chugged by. The train was a hit, and hundreds of millions of dollars in direct economic impact came to that corridor.

Twenty-five years of successful operation came to an end in 1999, when it became apparent that major work was needed to update the locomotive, and another new government did not provide the investment required. Despite studies demonstrating the value of the Hudson's immense positive economic impact on the region, no oil moved into the firebox, no fires were lit, no steam was generated, no drivers were turned, and the beauty sat silent again for more years.

No. 2860 was moved to the West Coast Railway Heritage Park (WCRHP) in 2002 to sit on permanent display amid a wide-ranging collection of railroad memorabilia. The park is home to more than ninety pieces of rolling stock sitting on various tracks— engines, working cars, passenger cars—along with station facilities, repair shops, and a recreated train station. Numerous displays provide insight into the workings of Canada's railways. Dedicated volunteers and members of the West Coast Railway Association maintain, repair, and exhibit their collection with immense pride, and the park welcomes tens of thousands of visitors every year who come to view the restored cars and marvel at the park's huge, new roundhouse.

In 2006, the locomotive went back in service, but only for a few short years on local trips, most notably to White Rock, BC, at the time of the 2010 Olympics Torch Run. No. 2860's certification expired in 2011, and many dollars are needed to continue its rebuilding and return it to operation. Fundraising efforts have been very successful, with plans to continue a ten-year rebuilding program that will cost more than $1 million.

Today, No. 2860 occupies a place of pride in the WCRHP Roundhouse, a dramatic reminder of its bygone glory days when it thrilled Canadians with its immense power and size.

ONE HELL OF A ROAR

YOUNG KETTLE VALLEY Railway trainman Alan Palm of Penticton, BC, had only been on the job one year when he experienced his singular claim to fame. It was a summer day in 1949, and his crew got a call to head down the Coquihalla Pass to Hope, BC, to pick up a circus train bound for Penticton. Arriving at Hope, they discovered that the train would need four engines to get back up the hill, so a second crew was called and the circus train was divided in two. Palm's train pulled flat cars carrying caged animals.

"As the wheels pounded out over the switch frog [the point in the switch where two rails cross], there was a hell of a roar, with a squirting sound, and I was covered from head to toe with lion shit!"

At dawn, the train stopped at a side track at Iago (northeast of Hope), and as daylight broke through, the lions bellowed, their magnificent roars eerily echoing across the canyon, while mountain goats raced up and down the cliffs in terror.

The engine crew forced Alan to ride on the back of the tender instead of in the cab because he stunk so bad.

THE TRAIN
WITH NO NAME

WHEN JIM MUNSEY, a supervisor with CN in Edmonton, arrived at work one morning in September 1969, he got a surprise. The general superintendent of transportation stood waiting for him and immediately summoned Munsey into his office.

"Close the door," said the superintendent in a hushed voice. "I need you to go back home immediately and pack your bags. Pack enough for five or six days on a train. Then book the first flight you can to Calgary. When you arrive, report to the regional manager of passenger services in the car foreman's office at Sarcee Yard."

"What's going on?" asked Jim anxiously.

The superintendent winced. "Sorry, I can't say. It's all secret. And by the way, don't tell anyone where you're going or for how long— not even your wife."

Jim drove home, intrigued by this mysterious assignment. He resisted his wife's attempt to know more. In his hurry to pack his bag, he forgot to remove a couple of signal fuses and three track torpedoes, little charges attached to a rail that explode as a locomotive's wheels pass over them, alerting the engineer that something's amiss ahead and they should slow down. (He used these for demonstration purposes at an orientation class he taught for newly employed trainmen.)

At the Edmonton airport, a security officer didn't like what she saw in the bag and summoned an RCMP constable, who confiscated the items and then allowed Jim on the plane. It was an ominous start to what was about to unfold.

It was late afternoon when he arrived outside the car foreman's office in Calgary. The passenger-services manager quickly hustled Jim into a secluded area of the rail yard.

"You're going to be interviewed by the King Security Agency of Los Angeles," he whispered. Once in the office, Jim watched incredulously as the interrogator sat busily reassembling a conductor's spectacle-mounted hearing aid. Apparently, he had taken it apart to ensure it was not a miniature radio transmitter.

Jim sank into a cracked wooden chair, trying desperately to appear calm as the interrogator peppered him with question after question. Yes, he'd worked for CN for twenty-five years. No, he didn't have a criminal record. Yes, he understood he could be fired for divulging anything he was about to see or hear.

The grilling over, the manager motioned Jim outside, where two diesel units, fourteen passenger cars, and a caboose were marshalled. Boxcars shielded the setup on adjacent tracks.

"Here's what I *can* tell you," began the manager furtively. "This train has been chartered by a special party who wants to remain anonymous. It doesn't have a set schedule, and its time of departure and destination will be withheld until the last possible moment.

"As the transportation officer, you are to ensure all pertinent operating rules, special instructions, and general instructions are properly observed. You'll also liaise between me and the train dispatchers on matters related to the movement of the train, and generally supervise the train and engine crew members.

"You'll be working with two others—CN's superintendent of transportation for Alberta, and the local trainmaster. The three of you are to share the supervisory duties for the coordination and operation of the train on a shift basis, and you're to be on the train at all times.

"Two mechanical supervisors have been assigned to ride the train to troubleshoot any electrical or mechanical problems that might occur," he added.

Jim's mind was already racing. A former train dispatcher, he was fully aware of the logistics involved in operating a train on short notice.

The manager continued. "The passenger cars will be fully staffed with sleeping and dining car personnel, and you are not to discuss the operation of the train with any of these employees. You'll sleep in an old colonist car at the head end. [Colonist cars had been used by immigrants to Canada and were a kind of train equivalent to travelling steerage on a ship.] You'll eat in the dining car during regular meal hours, but only after all the passengers have finished and are no longer present. If the train has stopped, you can only access the dining car from the outside. If the train is moving, you are to walk through the train to the diner, but you must not stop or make eye contact with any of the passengers. During the night, boxed lunches will be provided for the crew and supervisors directly from the dining car. Two special agents and a railway police constable have been assigned to protect the train and ensure the privacy of its occupants."

Jim's pleas for more information were useless, and he resigned himself to let his curiosity go unresolved. The manager, it seemed, would not divulge anything more and made it clear that only he would give directives.

"Our first directive came the next morning," recalled Jim. "We were instructed to run a short distance from the Sarcee Yard north to Conrich, where we were to stop and then return when so instructed. We pulled out of our hiding place—the train appearing normal, with a face visible in just about every passenger-car window—and twenty minutes later arrived at Conrich. We stopped on the main line, and off in the distance I could see three or four large clouds of dust on a country road. They were actually fast-moving limousines.

They parked beside the train, and several well-dressed gentlemen got out and hastily boarded the train. We later learned these men were senior officers of the various companies involved in a charter. They had arrived at the Calgary International Airport and were joining the rest of the group."

The train then returned to Sarcee Junction and yarded on a repair track, again with boxcars on both adjacent tracks. The supervisors and crew occupied themselves by reading, dozing, and eating, but at 9:00 p.m., they jumped into action when they received instructions to depart for Edmonton. On arriving there, the train was routed through to the Calder freight yard and onto the city loop track at West Junction. There, the dining and sleeping cars were restocked from the commissary.

"While walking back along the train, I was surprised to find the man from the King Security Company emptying the bags of soiled linen onto the platform," remembers Jim. "He was shaking out every piece before placing it back in the bag. He also went through the garbage bags from the dining and sleeping cars. We later learned he was looking for hidden notes or for anything that might provide information about the details or the purpose of the train."

Early the next morning, the train departed for Calgary. Jim already suspected that they were under heavy surveillance. Occupants of motor vehicles at some crossings behaved strangely. Someone had tipped off the news media that CN was operating a passenger train between Edmonton and Calgary under strange circumstances.

Even though the train was yarded where it could not be seen in Calgary, media were on to the story behind this "ghost" or "mystery train." Their vehicles (identifiable by logos) were parked on the perimeter of the yard. Railway employees arriving at or leaving the yard were bombarded with questions, all to no avail.

Private vehicles parked on the property attracted the media's attention.

"We were certain that media were using binoculars to record licence plate numbers in an effort to obtain clues as to the nature of the train," says Jim. But no detail had been overlooked by CN. Only rented cars were used by those directly involved with the train, and the rental company was obligated not to divulge any information about the identity of the drivers.

A new directive ordered another return trip to Conrich to pick up passengers arriving by air. Later that day, the train was ordered to make another return trip to Edmonton. Press cars followed the train on roads running parallel to the tracks, and could be seen frequently at public and private crossings. During the day, a helicopter hovered above and beside the train. To Jim, it was clear they were being watched through binoculars and being photographed with telescopic lenses.

Fresh supplies were loaded at Edmonton, and the security man again went through the laundry and garbage bags.

The media frenzy continued. While the sleeping and dining car staff were wearing their red waistcoats and from the outside could be seen going about their duties, from a distance they could be mistaken for the red tunics worn by the RCMP.

Some media reports alleged that US president Richard Nixon and North Vietnamese president Ho Chi Minh were on board, attempting to negotiate a peace treaty.

Jim and his colleagues played along with the secrecy. That evening, as he and the CN constable were standing on the north side of the yard, an aggressive newspaper reporter spotted the two and leapt at the opportunity to get the facts.

What would happen if one of the passengers got sick, he asked. Jim suggested that perhaps a doctor on board would help. What would happen if someone on board died? With the wink of an eye, Jim replied, "There is a deep freezer available in one of the cars where the body could be temporarily stored."

The reporter scoffed in frustration. "What would happen if I made a dash for the train?" The constable placed his hand on the butt of his .38 calibre revolver. "Try it!"

The next edition of that reporter's newspaper alleged the threat of gunplay, and the story generated national interest. The senior officers at headquarters in Montreal were not amused with the attention, and Jim and the constable were cautioned against further joviality with the media.

Later that evening, Jim spotted a van parked on the service road adjacent to the yard. A light flashed from a window, a light that Jim recognized was transmitting Morse code, but he couldn't take the time to translate what was being transmitted.

Newspaper headlines titillated fascinated readers: "Mystery Train Runs Under Tight Security"; "Modern Day Thriller, Spies, Secret Codes and All"; and "Mystery Train Guarded by Official Silence" were some of them.

"All of this attention became quite an adventure, and certainly relieved the monotony of babysitting a train," says Jim.

During the evening of the last full day the journey, Jim overheard a clandestine mobile-radio conversation coming from a van parked behind the yard office. "Two private jets at the Calgary International Airport could possibly have connections to the train. You are to follow any car seen leaving the Sarcee Yard." Jim reported this to one of the special police agents and said he knew of another route out of the yard that was seldom used and that led to a gravel road.

"Show me," commanded the agent. It was pitch-dark when the two climbed into a black rental car.

"The special agent put the car in gear, and as we began to move, I reminded him that he had forgotten to turn on the headlights," said Jim. "He told me that to avoid detection, he would not be using the headlights or applying brakes, so as not to illuminate the taillights. Recognizing my apprehension, he tried to give me peace of mind by telling me that before joining the railway, he had served on the morality squad of the Montreal Municipal Police and was accustomed to driving in the dark without lights. This was small comfort to me as we bounced over holes, bumps, old ties, and other debris until we finally reached the gravel road. We drove up and over the cattle guards at the crossing and entered the public road, headed towards the south. We began accelerating, and it was [so] dark I could barely see the hood ornament at the front of the car. After confirming this route would serve the purpose, we returned to the yard the same way. I was quite relieved to get back safely, and after regaining my composure, went to bed for a short sleep."

The next evening after sunset, the van with the mobile radio returned. "Be prepared to go to the airport on a moment's notice" instructed a voice to the driver. Overhearing this order, Jim chuckled. The van would not be going anywhere, because one of its back tires had mysteriously gone flat.

After dark, two selected vehicles left the yard for the airport on the road scouted the previous evening, with Jim riding in the second car, which was driven by a CN police constable. In each car rode two presumed senior officers of one of the companies and one other gentleman—all of whom carried briefcases possibly containing documents related to their work. Jim assumed that two sets of identical documents were being transported in the event one set was lost in an accident. Jim's vehicle followed the lead car to the airport. They were admitted to the tarmac and parked close to two executive jets. Two passengers transferred to the jets, which apparently were escorted by military-type aircraft to their destinations. The adventure was over, and by the next morning, the train was empty.

En route back to Edmonton, Jim walked through the vacated cars, noting the massive pile of items left behind—flip-chart sheets, notepaper on which was scribbled complicated formulas and geological surveys, yards of seismographic printouts and photos.

While there had been lots of excitement for people outside the train, for those sequestered inside the train, life was confining, to say the least. In his book *Treasurer-Seekers: The Men Who Built Home Oil*, author Philip Smith described the scene: "Men inside clustered around maps pinned in an empty baggage car or immersed in their calculations in smoke-filled compartments, unable to escape their imprisonment even long enough to call home." One executive, wrote Smith, apparently scrawled "Help" onto a laundry bag and flashed it to the eager reporters as the train moved through a station.

One of the trainmen—a railway historian—asked Jim if he'd kept all the train orders issued to them during the five days. He thought they'd be worth $2,500, given all the train's publicity. Jim said no, he hadn't kept them, as that was contrary to safe-operating procedures.

Just north of Mirror, a hamlet between Calgary and Edmonton, the exhausted supervisors gathered in one of the sleeper's smoking rooms. The conductor arrived, bearing several unopened shot bottles of whisky, enough for a couple of drinks each. After five nearly sleepless days aboard the mystery train, the whisky went down well. It was time to reflect on what they had only discovered the night before.

The reason for the secrecy came down to this: a consortium of thirteen small oil companies were eager to compete for some of the hundred or more leases on 1,036 hectares (2,560 acres) of the Prudhoe Bay oil field, which was being offered at an auction sale in Alaska. Espionage was common in the petroleum industry, and the consortium's executives wanted a secure place to analyze the potential of each parcel and to determine the maximum amount of their bid. They felt that meeting at conference facilities such as a hotel just wouldn't work, because professional and technical staff had too much idle time before and after making presentations, making them more vulnerable to outside influences. But a train would be ideal. As a cover for the covert operation and to avoid suspicion about the charter, the train had been chartered by the Hamilton Brothers Oil Company and code-named the Blue Sky Special.

Sipping their whisky, the supervisors knew they'd have amazing stories to tell friends and family at home. Can you imagine, they mused, that well before the train left Calgary that first day, the King Security Company had thoroughly scanned it for hidden listening and/or transmitting devices?

Finally at home and dead tired, Jim instantly fell asleep on a kitchen chair.

Later, the regional manager of passenger services held a "thank-you" dinner for the employees directly involved in the mystery train. He congratulated everyone on being so discreet and proudly proclaimed that the sequestered oil-company executives had successfully acquired most of the leases they wanted.

RAILWAY RUSE

TRAIN TRAVEL can be downright fun. No one knows this better than David Watts, a former railcar operator from Edmonton who in 1973 founded the Colonist Railcar Society (CRS), which bought and restored railway cars for adventure tours.

In 1975, two of the society's coaches were damaged by fire in a fuel delivery. CRS sued the agent, and after six years in court won a modest claim. In spring 1981, Watts decided to use some of the proceeds for a victory celebration for some society members, their lawyer, and his wife and daughter.

Why not, he mused, invite them on a free, round-trip, three-day excursion to Prince Rupert aboard his first-class 1931 sleeper (coupled to the end of VIA's train) on a route they'd never travelled before?

They leapt at the opportunity. Who could resist the thrill of riding in such historic elegance? This Canadian-built sleeper featured twelve open sections, with seats that faced each other and that converted to curtained upper and lower berths at night. The drawing room contained three beds and a private washroom. There was a men's smoking room with leatherette couches (now used as a lounge) and a women's powder room, converted to a kitchenette. They even had a shower in one of two public washrooms. The polished interior was finished with poplar plywood topped with Honduran mahogany panelling inlaid with ebony and rosewood borders on the berth frames and section partitions.

On the morning of their departure, Watts's fellow travellers convened in the railcar in high spirits, toting the very finest of liquid spirits to sustain them along the journey.

The conductor raised an eyebrow when he took their $6,000 ticket. Who were these people anyway? In the mid-1980s, this particular route was no tourist route. In fact, the government had declared it an "essential service." Loggers and local traffic were regular passengers on this run, not wealthy folks, like this group appeared to be. He was in awe.

Within minutes after leaving Edmonton, word quickly spread that millionaires were on board.

"They [the passengers on the VIA train] assumed we were millionaires—which we certainly were not—and started knocking on the door of our car to ask to look around," recalls Watts.

"We decided to play along, treating them to Courvoisier cognac VSOP and Harvey's Copper Beach—a special import a notch above Bristol Cream—sipped in the rear-end vestibule as we watched the tracks recede behind us.

"Our group included Canadians and others who were world-travelled, as well as a couple of artists and a symphonic composer. All this portrayed a somewhat exotic urbane-Bohemian-cross flair."

The ruse continued with style. At mealtime, Watts and his cohorts gleefully decided to act the part, and dressed for dinner: jackets, slacks, ties, and business suits for the men, dresses for the women. They entered the dining car to a chorus of hushed "oohs" and "ahs." (No tails or cocktail dresses—but still a definite contrast with the jeans and T-shirts worn by other passengers.)

This was ironic, because the other, "regular" passengers travelled in air-conditioned coaches (the 1931 sleeper was not) and slept on linens in berths made up by a porter. "Our group brought sleeping bags along and were self-contained, and we pulled down the berths ourselves," chuckles Watts.

The jig was eventually up when, in chatty "get-to-know-you" conversations that occur on such trips, it was discovered that the "millionaires" were really the hoi polloi that included teachers and nurses. "But still," says Watts in retrospect, "it was probably a mystery to them why we would have spent as much as we did on the fare simply to travel in our own private railcar."

On the return trip, they had an unexpected guest. Their train had to take the siding (a short section of track that trains could divert onto allow other trains to pass) for a freight that pulled alongside and stopped. An American woman scrambled off the caboose and boldly boarded the sleeper, not realizing it was private. She was a frequent rail traveller, too, who had persuaded the freight crew to carry her in the caboose until she became tired of the bumpy ride. When they told her they were about to pass a passenger train, she decided to try her luck on that. The conductor on this trip—somewhat officious-looking, with a toothbrush mustache—marched back to the sleeper, irritated at the unscheduled stop and the fact that she didn't have a ticket.

"Since our travel was paid for on a per-car, not a per-passenger basis, we were free to carry anyone, short of a wanted criminal, with us," says Watts. "So we extended her political asylum, the miffed conductor departed, and the train went on its way. Had the conductor intercepted her before she was received aboard our car, he would have had more control of the situation. Since she didn't know, before changing trains, that our car was privately owned, I'm sure she was prepared to pay the going coach fare at least."

Watts can't recall whether she eventually paid or not. It didn't really matter, though she could well afford to. She owned a few houses in upstate New York, and she invited the cozy cabal in the first-class sleeper to visit her there—perhaps for more adventures.

WOMEN AT WORK—AND
PLAY—ON THE RAILROAD

IN THE TWENTIETH century, many Canadian male railroaders fondly penned gripping stories about their on-the-job adventures. Replete with bravado, hardships, and camaraderie, their writing seldom mentioned women, other than the occasional "she" (as an affectionate reference to a locomotive) or a train station named after a woman—perhaps after a railway owner's daughter. Male train historians wrote equally compelling books. So, where were the stories written by or about women? Despite little opportunity to work for railway companies and develop the passion shared by train buffs, trains did excite the female imagination.

Before the First World War, few women would have hummed the old American folk song, "I've Been Working on the Railroad." But the line "Just to pass the time away" never applied to the women who successfully took over the physically demanding work previously done by the men who had gone overseas to fight in the First and Second World Wars.

During the Second World War, CPR hired women to work as engine wipers and car cleaners. At its roundhouse at Alyth yards in Calgary, women in blue overalls scrambled up and over locomotives, responding with pride to the federal government's plea to women to "roll up your sleeves for victory!"

In an issue of the *Penticton Herald* in 1943, a reader asked, in a letter to the editor, "What do my eyes see this morning?" He was writing about seeing women working in the rail yard that was the

Jessie Carter (right) and friend start their shift to check tracks in and around Penticton.

hub of the Kettle Valley Railway. The letter went on, "Actually, some of our local girls [are] doing a man-sized job cleaning the tracks, working with a will. Nothing glamorous about the looks of them. From here I can see two of them in khaki overalls, hair piled in under the striped railway cap with sweat and dust as their main make-up."

Sledge wielders, track heavers, pick-and-shovel artists—they were all this and more.

One such woman was Jessie Carter, a vibrant twenty-year-old Penticton resident who, along with her workmates, cleaned switches, lit lamps every evening, and maintained railway ties. To replace a section of rail meant hoisting a twelve-metre-long (thirty-nine-foot) piece of steel weighing thirty-nine kilograms (eighty-five pounds). The women dug ditches, weeded the rail yard, and painted loco-motives, in the process, getting fit and enjoying the work. Engine cleaning, it seemed, was much more interesting than the typical women's work they had done in the past.

Jessie Carter repairing tracks in CPR yards, Penticton. JESSIE CARTER FORMO COLLECTION

In the summer, Jessie and eleven other women on the crew iced boxcars of fruit. About two hundred cars full of ice were brought in from Keith, Alberta, and stored in Penticton. At peak times, fifty cars a day were fully iced and another thirty-five re-iced.

Part of the work involved standing on a 180-kilogram (400-pound) ice "cake" atop a refrigerator car and shovelling the ice in. Each car required 3,175 to 3,630 kilograms (7,000 to 8,000 pounds) of ice to reduce the temperature to 2°C (35°F). From Penticton, the iced cars were routed to Haynes, loaded with crated peaches that had been trucked from Osoyoos, and then returned to Penticton, and possibly re-iced, before being loaded on two barges to be taken north up Okanagan Lake to Kelowna by CPR tugs.

WHEN LADY SUSAN Agnes Macdonald, the second wife of Canada's first prime minister, Sir John A. Macdonald, joined her husband on their first journey west across Canada aboard the newly completed CPR line, the spirited fifty-year-old was smitten by train travel. The engineer and fireman were happy to answer her many train-related questions, and even allowed her to sound a whistle. But they were not amused when, nearing the Rockies at Laggan (Lake Louise), she insisted on riding in the cowcatcher. Trembling at the very thought of this outrageous act, and realizing that arguing against it was futile, the crew quickly found a candle-box for her to sit on, and placed it in the buffer-beam.

The buffer-beam, as Lady Macdonald described, "is that narrow, heavy iron platform, with the sides scooped out, as it were, on the very forefront of the engine, over which the headlight glares. The description of a cowcatcher is less easy. To begin with, it is mis-named, as it catches no cows at all... it clears the line by shoving forward, or tossing aside, any removable obstruction. It is best described as a sort of barred iron beak, about six feet long, projecting over the track in a V shape, and attached to the buffer-beam by very strong bolts."

As the train snorted out of Laggan, a gaggle of horrified onlookers couldn't hide their disapproval. Lady Macdonald cared not.

"'It is an awful thing to do!' I hear a voice say, as the little group lean forward; and for a moment I feel a thrill that is very like fear; but it is gone at once, and I can think of novelty, the excitement, and the fun of this mad ride in glorious sunshine and intoxicating air, with magnificent mountains before and around me, their lofty peaks smiling down on us, and never a frown on their grand faces!"

The train chuffed to the summit at the Great Divide and eventually through Kicking Horse River Valley and a thrilling descent 853 metres (2,800 feet) over 19 kilometres (12 miles) through the mountain wilderness in British Columbia. Lady Macdonald was mesmerized.

CN rail employees escort train hoppers to rail offices in Foleyet, Ontario. The Ontario Provincial Police later issued trespassing fines. ZOE MCKNIGHT

"I could only gaze at the glaciers that the mountains held so closely," she wrote, "5,000 feet [1,524 metres] above us, at the trace of snow avalanches which had left a space a hundred feet wide massed with torn and prostrate trees; on the shadows that played over the distant peaks; and on a hundred rainbows made by the foaming, dashing river, which swirls with tremendous rapidity down the gorge on its way to the Columbia in the valley below. There is glory of brightness and beauty everywhere, and I laugh aloud on the cowcatcher, just because it is all so delightful!"

The exquisite experience evidently left an impression on her, so much so that her zeal for cowcatcher riding attracted the imagination of other women. Riding a cowcatcher soon became a sought-after activity, and Lady Macdonald passionately wrote about her travels in magazine articles.

It's quite probable that intrepid journalist Zoe McKnight would have got on famously with Lady Macdonald. Too bad their kindred spirits were separated by adventures 121 years apart.

In 2007, twenty-three-year-old Zoe and her boyfriend fantasized about train-hopping across Canada. "Riding the rails is part of our country's history. It sounded so romantic," she recalls. "I thought it would be a great adventure." Indeed, it was: dangerous and exciting, and like Lady Macdonald's escapade, illegal.

Late one August evening, Zoe and her boyfriend snuck into the CN rail yards a few kilometres outside Sudbury, Ontario. A westbound freight train loaded with some fifteen-metre-long (forty-eight-foot) intermodals on flatcars was about to pull out. (Intermodals are rectangular-shaped shipping containers that make it possible to move freight on different modes of transportation interchangeably.)

Stealthily, the pair opened an unlocked and empty intermodal. They stowed their backpacks—stuffed with a Bunsen burner, two canisters of fuel, tofu, red peppers, bottled water, chocolate-covered almonds, and cans of beans—and unrolled sleeping bags onto the sawdust-covered, debris-strewn floor. Outside on the platform at the end of the intermodal, they hid under a tarp. As dawn broke, the freight grunted, shuddered, and thundered out of the yard. The fantasy journey was on!

About an hour later, they were pulled off the train by "bulls" (railway police) who discovered Zoe, her partner, and two other train hoppers under the tarp. The group was escorted to CN offices in nearby Foleyet, Ontario, a community built around the CN line.

Undeterred by the $120 fine for trespassing, Zoe and her partner hitchhiked to a rail yard near Lake Superior. There, they climbed into the blackness of another empty intermodal and "caught out" (train-hoppers' lingo) for the West.

Could hiding in an unventilated, dark, and dirty shipping container be fun? Time would tell.

"At every stop, we were super quiet; not saying a word and listening for the voices of railway employees with their walkie-talkies crackling right outside," remembers Zoe. Amazingly, they encountered no more security after Northern Ontario.

There was constant clanging, banging, and vibrations; and there was no sleep. A bitterly cold night through Manitoba was followed by ten wretched hours baking in their "steel tent" when the train stopped near Moose Jaw, Saskatchewan. Exhausted and dehydrated, Zoe and her boyfriend eventually made a mad dash across a field to the Trans-Canada Highway, where they got a ride to a grocery store for water.

Despite the dirt and danger, the romantic notion of train hopping was still very much alive. They never contemplated giving up. Getting stuck, getting caught, and having to make on-the-fly changes to the original plan were part of the adventure. They hitchhiked to Calgary, but weren't about to try the yard there, so jumped on a bus to Field, BC. For hours, they waited until another freight train finally stopped in its tracks.

In the early afternoon, they "disappeared" into another intermodal on a train headed for Vancouver. Near Rogers Pass, in the Selkirk Mountains, the freight approached the fourteen-and-a-half-kilometre-long (nine-mile) Mount Macdonald Tunnel, the longest railway tunnel in the western hemisphere.

Inside the tunnel, standing on the ledge of the railcar, Zoe felt trapped in a surreal situation.

"Imagine the sounds: the high-pitched squeal of the rails is amplified because you're in a tunnel. Other than some security lighting high up, it was pitch-dark. We had to cover our mouths with bandanas because soot was flying everywhere," says Zoe. "I realized that if anything went wrong, we had no escape. No one would ever find us. No one had any idea we were on this train."

The Columbia River, seen from an intermodal somewhere near the BC–Alberta border.
ZOE MCKNIGHT

Zoe and her boyfriend decided to get off at the Port Coquitlam rail yards rather than at Vancouver, where there was likely to be more security personnel. Groggy after five days without sleep, and layered in grime, Zoe and her boyfriend crawled out of the intermodal, squinting in the early dawn light, and staggered up a nearby ridge covered in blackberry bushes that bordered a golf course.

The adventure was over, eagerly celebrated with coffees at a roadside stand and a bus ride into Vancouver, where Zoe bought a much-needed change of clothes.

Looking back, Zoe says the magnificent scenery was the best part. In unpopulated areas, with fewer chances of being seen by railway police, she boldly hung out on a platform outside the inter-modal. How exhilarating to savour the Canadian Shield, lakes, trees, prairie, rivers, and mountains in the fresh air rather than from inside a car.

She also noted that train hopping is illegal and dangerous. You don't want to get on or off of a moving train. Being in a tunnel is dangerous, and there's no one to go to if you need help. There's no cell service, so if anything happens, there's no opportunity to call for help.

"I heard horror stories of people who woke up in the Winnipeg yard while their shipping container was being lifted by crane, and they had to make a run for it rather than getting stuck on a trip to China," she says.

"Train hopping is even more dangerous for women," she adds. "An unaccompanied woman would be unsafe the entire time. A lot of people ride the rails as a form of transportation rather than enter-tainment, and they are not necessarily the type you want to meet when your defences are down."

Convicted train hoppers can face thousands of dollars in fines and time in jail.

Would Lady Macdonald have approved? Outwardly, probably not. But secretly, she might have admired the tenacity of a young woman who resolved to live out her fantasy—and who got away liv-ing it on a section of Mr. Macdonald's railway.

WHISTLE POST FIVE
RIDING THE RAILS
INTO THE FUTURE

IS THERE A future for rail travel in this age so far advanced from that when railroads were considered new and essential? It would seem so. While the options for means of travel are more numerous than ever, rail may have real potential in the realms of tourism and in offering alternatives to an unsustainable auto culture. Light rapid transit for suburban communities, and attractive rail routes for tourists, Canadian and international alike, are two such modern uses for rail travel.

◄ The Rocky Mountaineer has been called "the most spectacular train trip in the world" and here passes through remarkable scenery on one of its four routes. ROCKY MOUNTAINEER™ IS A TRADEMARK OF THE GREAT CANADIAN RAILTOUR COMPANY LTD.

THE MOUNTAINEER

"IF WE CAN'T export the scenery, we'll import the tourists," said William Van Horne. It was 1888. The American railroader from Illinois was serving as president of the CPR, and the scenery he was talking about was the majestic Rocky Mountain range. Having carved through the mountains, around them, over and alongside them while building Canada's national railway, Van Horne was convinced they would appeal to visitors from around the world, and the only way to get there was on his train. What began as a railway company focused on moving freight and people soon grew to include iconic chateau-style hotels at sites chosen by Van Horne. The Banff Springs Hotel was one of them; Victoria's Empress was another.

A hundred years later, Van Horne's vision would be further expanded by two modern railroaders who had a dream of their own. Van Horne's new partners-in-vision were Harry Home and Pat Crowley.

Home and Crowley shared a fascination for steam trains and were involved with Steam Expo, a gathering in Vancouver in 1986 that saw all manner of steam locomotives arrive as a prelude to Expo '86, the World Exposition on Transportation and Communication. With the world spotlight focused on BC, Horne and Crowley contrived to fill heritage coaches with dignitaries and tourists. Pulled by Bullet Nose Betty, a renowned steam locomotive from 1944, the train would take her passengers from Jasper to Vancouver. The novelty of their idea was that the train would only travel by daylight, a plan that would guarantee travellers an unparalleled visual experience.

Accomplishing this meant that travellers would disembark in Kamloops for an overnight stay before continuing their journey (and the Jasper-to-Vancouver route would also stop overnight in Kamloops to ensure "all daylight" travel).

With that notion (more complex that it might seem), Home and Crowley laid the foundation for a successful, world-famous train experience. Today, travel by train to Banff (Jasper's southern sister in the Rockies), is exclusively on the Rocky Mountaineer. It was not always so. Provenance for that train's name goes back to 1923, when the Mountaineer first figured in Western Canada's railway lore.

The first incarnation of the Mountaineer through the Canadian Rockies was under the purview of the Soo Line. (The sobriquet "the Soo" was taken from the phonetic spelling of the French word *Sault* in the name Minneapolis, St. Paul and Sault Ste. Marie Railroad. Today, the CPR owns the Soo Line.) The Mountaineer operated from Chicago to Vancouver via Minneapolis–St. Paul, in cooperation with the CPR. Trains moved travellers north and west 260 kilometres (roughly 160 miles) on tracks built by the CPR across Minnesota to North Dakota's growing town of Portal. This enabled a connection with Saskatchewan's city of Moose Jaw, where passenger coaches were coupled onto the CPR's cross-Canada train heading to Alberta and farther west.

The route from Chicago to Minneapolis to Canada and the Rockies was not always the now-internationally known Calgary–Banff–Vancouver corridor through Rogers Pass. An earlier iteration of this journey, at the start of the 1900s, went through the more southern Canadian Rockies, stopping in Fernie, using the Crowsnest Pass to Cranbrook, then veering south to Idaho before venturing to Spokane in Washington State and across to Oregon. This was known as the Soo–Spokane–Portland Train Deluxe until it was discontinued in 1914.

Later, the Soo-Pacific was registered in the early 1920s. The sleeping-car only, summer-season train became The Mountaineer shortly thereafter. It was owned by two separate companies, one in the US and one in Canada. Deluxe coaches from the Pullman Sleeping Car Company and an assortment of exquisite dining rooms and parlour cars enhanced its reputation. Eventually, impressive observation cars were added at the end of the trains. Legend has it that Al Capone rode the Mountaineer out of Chicago heading to Moose Jaw, where underground tunnels were used to hide and transport illegal alcohol during Prohibition (perhaps assisted by a railroad). Today, Moose Jaw plays up the rumours of Capone sightings for tourists with the Tunnels of Moose Jaw attraction. His visit to the town remains unproven—but then, so do many of his alleged murders.

This train service was a popular way to cross from the US Midwest to Vancouver—as much for the awesome scenery as for the convenience. It was well used for years until it was faced with decreasing passenger numbers and increasing costs—even as efficiencies were implemented. The last steam locomotive was used on the line in 1959, and the route was terminated in summer 1960.

Even though the Mountaineer and the Canadian Rockies had become associated in the minds of international railway travellers, the train, and the brand, went into hibernation. For twenty-eight years, the moniker "mountaineer" was absent from the Rocky Mountains except in describing intrepid climbers, explorers, and hikers.

That all changed in 1986, when Harry Home and Pat Crowley's proposal for daylight train service from the Rockies to Vancouver, beginning in Jasper on the CN tracks, breathed new life into the concept. They called their fledgling train company Rocky Mountain Rail Inc. and named their train Jasper by Daylight. Homes says, "We planned on using the 6060, Bullet Nose Betty, for short distances, on special occasions." The idea for all-daylight travel only for the two-day trip was new and fresh, and it was theirs alone. Their first step was to get the proposal in front of CN executives. Crowley had prepared a detailed itinerary, and the entire tour was plotted out in preparation for their presentation. They were brushed off and shunted to VIA Rail. As Home told author Paul Grescoe in an interview years later, "They never replied to us."

In what seemed to be a coincidental stroke of marketing brilliance, competition sprang on Home and Crowley. As Home told Grescoe, "Suddenly VIA made a hurry-up announcement that they were going to run this train from Jasper to Vancouver." The owners of Rocky Mountain Rail were flummoxed. Home tallied the comparisons: "The schedule, the timing, the sleeping-over in Kamloops..." The litany of similarities between the newly forged VIA service and the Home/Crowley proposal continued. Home let it be known that they were exasperated. "We did consider going to court," he said. Instead, they let it play out. Home and Crowley stood aside. It all seemed to boil down to a new marketing concept falling into the hands of those who had the resources to make it happen versus those who needed help to find funding and support.

VIA Rail is a crown corporation created in 1977 by the federal government as Canada's national passenger service, acquiring all of CN's passenger cars and locomotives and, in 1978, all of the CPR's. VIA Rail's service replaced the two national railways' money-losing passenger trains, the Canadian and the Super Continental. Passenger trains were shunted aside on timetables to make room for the more profitable freight trains. For VIA, this meant their passengers were asleep when their trains passed through some of the country's most spectacular scenery, the Rockies. Some would stay awake in the dark hours, struggling to see the magnificent peaks by night; periodically they would be rewarded with a moonlit spectacle or a star-graced setting. Visitors expected more.

VIA's 1988 solution was a new, two-day rail tour focused on the Rockies, stopping overnight in Kamloops so that passengers could see the amazing mountains in all their splendour. VIA called their new excursion Rockies by Daylight. It was then rechristened the Rocky Mountaineer, a name that borrowed from the history books. It was the rebirth of a brand and a fledgling venture that rekindled Van Horne's farsighted pledge to make the Rockies accessible for rail travellers.

With cost considerations at the forefront for the government of the day, VIA's subsidy, staff, equipment, and schedules were all subject to budget cuts at the end of the 1980s. As part of a recasting of the corporation, the federal government decided in 1990 to privatize the Rocky Mountaineer, putting it up for sale in a competitive tender. Many international buyers expressed interest, and a bidding process winnowed these down to three notable candidates, eventually selecting one to whom they sold their daylight Rockies service.

Peter Armstrong, along with investors and railroad experts, took over the daylight train service and its uncertain future. At first, it was called Mountain Vistas Rail Services, which then changed to Great Canadian Railtours, finally becoming, once more, the Rocky Mountaineer. In more recent years, under the stewardship of president and CEO Randy Powell, the Rocky Mountaineer has gained a great reputation in the world of train travel.

VIA Rail's The Canadian today offers the only cross-Canada train service, which begins its Rockies-bound journey in Toronto, then continues to Winnipeg and to the northwest through Edmonton–Jasper–Vancouver, a remnant, though still significant, of the original transcontinental service. Together, VIA Rail and the Rocky Mountaineer offer Western Canada's magnificent scenery to the world.

In a brand-name competition that the owners of either railway never envisioned, the Rocky Mountaineer nears the world-famous Orient Express in media mentions and traveller recognition. The

ROCKY MOUNTAINEER RAILTOURS®   ROCKY MOUNTAINEER

Shown here are three iconic rail logos that have aligned the name "Mountaineer" with trains that travelled through the Canadian Rockies: The Mountaineer (1923–1960); The Rocky Mountaineer, Great Canadian Railtours (1990–2006); and Rocky Mountaineer Armstrong Group, (2006–present). ROCKY MOUNTAINEER™ IS A TRADEMARK OF THE GREAT CANADIAN RAILTOUR COMPANY LTD.

Rocky Mountaineer has already matched and in some ways surpassed the Orient Express's onboard cuisine, calibre of wines, and traveller-acknowledged attendant expertise and service. The two train experiences today co-define "best known train names." Perhaps, in the coming decades, the home-grown Rocky Mountaineer may surpass the cachet of the Orient Express on the brand-recognition track—quite the change from the days the Soo Line was the custodian of the Mountaineer. Harry Home and Pat Crowley, take a bow!

INTERURBANATION

THERE'S NO SUCH word, of course, as interurbanation, but maybe there should be: it's been coined here to describe the story of a venerable short-line railway that has been in operation for more than a century. Few Western Canadians would think much of these smaller operators, focusing more on the coast-to-coast giants that realized our national dreams. But one, in the southwest corner of BC, has its own place in local history.

The lush greenery of the Fraser Valley leads eastward from the Greater Vancouver area, with Simon Fraser's namesake river winding peacefully through it past rich and productive farmland, forested slopes, and bustling valley communities. Through this fertile landscape, up steep hills and down into swampy hollows, you'll find tracks with tales to tell.

The population of the valley has soared close to a million now, with most living south of the Fraser River. Every day, many residents leave their homes for the long commute to work or other appointments in the urban metropolis comprising Metro Vancouver. For the most part, they drive vehicles.

Commuter rail once served many larger population centres in the valley south of the river, and modern concepts have been demonstrated, tested, and proven, according to proponents, and yet this approach to moving thousands of people every day is seemingly unattainable. Many valley residents wonder why. The tracks are there, for the most part. Upgrading is required, of course, but rights-of-way and routing have been in place in one form or another since the first interurban railways started in this part of the world in 1890.

The modern interurban phenomenon of SkyTrain has been a huge success for BC's Greater Vancouver area. Three lines with 300 rail vehicles, 47 stations, and over 60 kilometres (37 miles) of track deliver around 400,000 people to a wide variety of locations every day. With the building of the Evergreen line to Coquitlam and other extensions and lines under development, SkyTrain's impact on Vancouver is huge.

The West Coast Express has proven successful as well. Trains start each morning in Mission on the north side of the Fraser River and travel to downtown Vancouver in seventy-seven minutes. The return trips bring commuters home to valley communities in late afternoon. Estimates suggest the Express has reduced road traffic in amounts exceeding 4,000 cars per day, with the commensurate effect of reducing greenhouse gases in the environment by more than 21,000 tons each day.

But what of the hundreds of thousands of people who live in valley communities south of the river, more than 120,000 of whom use the Port Mann Bridge on Highway 1 every day?

Answers may lie in the more recent history of Fraser Valley transportation, starting with the creation of the British Columbia Electric Railway Company (BCER) in 1897. Earlier efforts at establishing electric railways in Victoria, Vancouver, and New Westminster had started in 1890, but the companies had met with economic challenges, financial difficulties, and technical problems. Then entrepreneur Robert Horne-Payne established the BCER from the ashes of those earlier companies and brought together investors who would make interurban rail a reality. New dams in the mountainous regions of the Lower Mainland generated electricity to power these lines. Facilities were established to build cars for the expanding rail links across the growing suburban landscape. Early in the first decade of the twentieth century, an interurban line from New

Westminster to Chilliwack was announced and was open for business in 1910. Other lines sprung up across the Lower Mainland, and in time, the Interurban system became the largest in Canada, with several multi-car trains running the length of the system every day.

Early commuters rode those rails to jobs closer to Vancouver. Families travelled into the urban core to reach entertainment venues and big-city adventures. In some consists, freight cars delivered goods along the way as well as passengers. Milk was a major commodity moved along the tracks, transported from dairy farms in the valley to local stations and from there throughout the metropolitan area. A "milk train" departed from Chilliwack every morning at 7:00 a.m. and stopped along the way to pick up milk cans from farmers. Its arrival in New Westminster by 10:00 a.m. allowed those cans filled with fresh milk to be distributed to dairies in New Westminster for processing. Farm produce, locally fabricated material, products from lumber mills, mail, and other goods were transported from Chilliwack, the easternmost population centre in the valley, westward along a meandering route through smaller places like Sardis and Yarrow, and to Huntingdon, at the us border. The trains continued north through Abbotsford and to Milner Station, then across to Langley Prairie, Cloverdale, Newton, and Surrey, and ultimately to New Westminster.

With cars and trucks being used increasingly for transporting people and goods, change came to the Interurban landscape within a couple of decades. Slowly but surely, the metropolitan area saw the emergence of motorbuses, and Interurban use plummeted. Line after line lost its customer base, and eventually service was reduced and then cancelled as traffic moved "from rails to rubber." The familiar sound of Interurban horns coming to a crossing faded into obscurity.

Interurban service between New Westminster and Chilliwack continued to operate into the 1950s, transporting freight as well as passengers. But the valley population was growing dramatically, too,

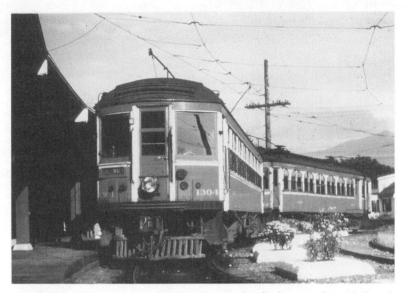

In 1950, a BC Electric two-car Interurban train readies for departure from Chilliwack, heading to New Westminster. Car 1304 is being restored today.

GEOFF MEUGENS, HENRY EWERT COLLECTION, FRASER VALLEY HERITAGE RAILWAY SOCIETY

and new and expanded highway connections facilitated road traffic. In time, the number of users of the Interurban service declined to the point where it could no longer be justified.

Soon, the sound of diesel engines replaced the quiet electric cars, and diesel-led consists continued to transport freight throughout the valley. Ownership changes came when the provincial government took over the BCER in 1960 and created the British Columbia Hydro and Power Authority (BC Hydro). Eventually, the rail system was sold again and became the Southern Railway of British Columbia, or SRY, the name it continues to operate under today.

With almost one hundred kilometres of main-line track in service today, the Southern Railway moves a wide variety of products along its line, including general freight, cars and trucks, consumer goods, machinery, chemicals, and commodities. Twenty-nine locomotives and more than seven hundred cars comprise the railway's consists. The company cites a customer base of over a hundred and fifty suppliers.

Still, the clamoring for a return to interurban transport of people resonates in the valley. Commuters on the south of the river point to the success of the West Coast Express and ask "Why not here?" Demonstration lines have been operated a few times over the years, generally with success. Vancouver's hugely successful Expo '86 was originally conceived as Transpo '86, with a focus on transportation, but while the focus of Expo broadened, the transportation element was the foundation of a major event that brought the Greater Vancouver area worldwide recognition (and that brought SkyTrain's first line, the Expo line). A demonstration line between Abbotsford and New Westminster proved to be a very popular part of the fair's theme, and while it came to an end with the closing of Expo in October of that year, the point was well made: light-rail transit is a viable option for the south side of the Fraser River. Fairgoers used it, but so did commuters, once the option was available.

Rail for the Valley is an organized group actively championing new services that can address the perceived demand south of the river. The positions for and against commuter rail generate a huge amount of controversy. Provincial government studies say the timing is not right to spend public funds on light-rail rapid transit for the area, yet local government leaders speak out in favour of it. Media editorials often support the cause as well. Leading local politicians such as former Surrey mayor Dianne Watts address it positively, saying, "South of the Fraser, we want at-grade light rail. You see it all over the world." Advocates suggest that government studies are flawed, and international experts have confirmed the viability of such services. They cite construction cost comparisons that put the price of implementing a light-rail system on existing publicly owned rights-of-way at $5 million per kilometre (a little over half a mile), whereas costs of building SkyTrain routes normally approach $140 million per kilometre.

These issues have been fodder for conspiracy theories. Debates rage even today about the role of major companies, led by General Motors, in changing the landscape of major cities across the continent from being served by interurban railways of one sort or another to being served by buses. Were the first years of massive highway construction just a "time of life" in North America, or was there some grand scheming behind it all? Opinions are divided, usually quite sharply, and BC's decades-long success with interurban transportation carries its own theorists on both sides of this controversial question.

For the most part, the tracks and rights-of-way from the old Interurban that ran from New Westminster to Chilliwack are intact. While freight traffic comprises 100 percent of its operations today, Southern Railway operates only a few trains each day, leaving the tracks available for potential interurban passenger services much of the time. Will this continue to be the case, or might commuters and other Lower Mainland residents south of the Fraser someday be able to avoid clogged highways and reach their destinations by light rapid transit?

Questions will continue to be raised from various corners, including whether the existing tracks, which dodge and weave their way through the valley, will be suitable for modern commuter rail or whether a completely new route is required, making the proposition a far more daunting and expensive challenge. And if the tracks are devoted to passenger transit, what of the resulting increases of traffic on other existing rail lines in the valley, particularly with coal traffic destined for Roberts Bank?

Resolution to these issues is a long way off, and in the meantime the freight trains continue to roll on those same rights-of-way.

Perhaps one day, they will carry passengers again, bringing some much-needed relief to this road-congested region and providing commuters and families a pleasant, efficient, and clean way to reach their destinations.

AFTERWORD

TRAINS ARE HERE to stay. As this book goes to press, high-speed rail developments are on the drawing boards in numerous countries—expansions of existing services or new builds. In Western Canada, there's a perennial push for a high-speed rail link connecting Edmonton with Calgary and dreams of a high-speed rail corridor between Vancouver and Seattle.

For traditional freight or dangerous cargo, rail will remain a preferred (though certainly not risk-averse) mode of transportation. The environmental benefits of rail will increasingly compare favourably vis-à-vis airlines, motor carriers, and ships along the coast.

It's also exciting that railway tourism is on the increase. Rail museums and restored steam locomotives attract thousands of train aficionados every year. We've featured some of these enduring attractions in this book; we encourage you to visit and explore them. They're marvellous windows into our history. Modern train consists, providing some of the best "live steam" experiences in the world, call Western Canada home.

We hope that our stories, which generally span the last 125 years, have entertained you and captured your imagination. But we wonder, how might train stories of the twenty-first century differ from the ones we've told in *Whistle Posts West*? Will future storytellers marvel at a one-hour ride between Calgary and Edmonton, at speeds of up to 240 kilometres (150 miles) per hour? Will the rapidly growing population of BC's Fraser Valley have rapid-rail access from Hope westward into Vancouver? What new adventures await travellers on

A heritage steam train visits McClean Mill National Heritage Site in Port Alberni, BC.
NICHELE PORTRAIT STUDIO

a transcontinental train as it snakes its way across Canada, taking travellers through the majestic Rocky Mountains? Could new discoveries of gold in Yukon once again beckon thrill seekers who arrive by train? What new technology will enable trains to transport environmentally sensitive goods safely to west-coast ports?

Many readers no doubt have their own railway stories to tell. If you are one of them, we encourage you to contact a railway museum and share your stories for future generations to enjoy.

Now, our conductor is calling and our train is pulling out from the station. All aboard!

WESTERN CANADA RAIL EXPERIENCES

RESIDENTS AND VISITORS to Western Canada today have a number of options to ride the rails on scenic or heritage tours, or to see steam trains, static railway displays, and places that exude railroad history. Here are some that are worth a visit:

BRITISH COLUMBIA

Alberni Pacific "Steam" Railway
Alberni Valley Heritage Network
Port Alberni, BC
alberniheritage.com

The Canadian Museum of Rail Travel
Cranbrook, BC
trainsdeluxe.com

Creston Museum
Creston, BC
creston.museum.bc.ca

Fort Steele Railway Co.
Fort Steele Heritage Town

Fort Steele, BC
fortsteele.ca

Kaoham Shuttle
Seaton Lake, Lillooet, BC
tsalalh.net/shuttle.html
exploregoldcountry.com

Kamloops Heritage Railway
Kamloops, BC
kamrail.com/

Kettle Valley Steam Railway
Summerland, BC
kettlevalleyrail.org

Revelstoke Railway Museum
Revelstoke, BC
railwaymuseum.com

Rocky Mountaineer
Vancouver, BC
rockymountaineer.com

West Coast Railway
    Heritage Park
Squamish, BC
wcra.org

Kimberley's Underground
    Mining Railway
Kimberley, BC
kimberleysunderground-
    miningrailway.ca

Three Valley Gap Heritage
    Ghost Town
Three Valley Gap, BC
3valley.com

VIA Rail Canada
viarail.ca

ALBERTA
Alberta Prairie Railway
    Excursions
Stettler, Alberta
absteamtrain.com/

Edmonton, Yukon &
    Pacific Railway
Fort Edmonton Park,
Edmonton, Alberta
fortedmontonpark.ca

Heritage Park
    Historic Village
Calgary, Alberta
heritagepark.ca

YUKON
Copperbelt Railway &
    Mining Museum
Whitehorse, Yukon
yukonrails.com
White Pass & Yukon Route
    Railway, Canadian
    terminus
wpyr.com

ALASKA
White Pass & Yukon
    Route Railway, American
    terminus
Skagway, Alaska
wpyr.com

SOURCES

THE AUTHORS HAVE consulted a variety of sources for this book. As often happens with history, there is likely to be conflicting information and interpretation among sources. Where there were differing views or conflicting information, we made decisions with which we were comfortable.

BOOKS

Anderson, Frank W. *Bill Miner, Stagecoach and Train Robber*. Surrey, BC: Heritage House, 1982.

Gibbon, John Murray. *The Romantic History of the Canadian Pacific: The Northwest Passage of Today*. New York: Van Res Press, 1935.

Grescoe, Paul. *Trip of a Lifetime: The Making of the Rocky Mountaineer*. Vancouver: Douglas & McIntyre, 2005.

Ingram, Rob. *White Pass and Yukon Route Railway: An Historical Survey*. Great Plains Research Consultants, 1988.

Klinck, Carl F. *Robert Service*. New York: Dodd, Mead & Co., 1976.

Lavallée, Omer. *Van Horne's Road: The Building of the Canadian Pacific Railway*. Markham, ON: Fitzhenry & Whiteside, 2007.

Liddell, Ken. *I'll Take the Train*. Saskatoon: Western Producer Prairie Books, 1966.

McKee, Bill, and Georgeen Klassen. *Trail of Iron: The CPR and the Birth of the West*. Vancouver: The Glenbow–Alberta Institute and Douglas & McIntyre, 1983.

MacBeth, R.G. *The Romance of the Canadian Pacific Railway*. Toronto: Ryerson Press, 1924.

Macdonald, Susan Agnes. *By Cow and by Cowcatcher,* pp. 114–18, in *Tales from the Canadian Rockies,* Brian Patton, ed. Toronto: McClelland & Stewart, 1993.

Minter, Roy. *The White Pass: Gateway to the Klondike.* Toronto: McClelland & Stewart, 1987.

Palm, Alan. *Lions in the Coquihalla.* Penticton, BC: Privately printed, 1988.

Pratt, E. J. *Towards the Last Spike.* Toronto: MacMillan, 1952.

Service, Robert. *The Spell of the Yukon and Other Poems.* New York: Dodd, Mead and Company, 1907, 1916.

———. *Ploughman of the Moon. An Adventure into Memory.* New York: Dodd & Company, Mead, 1945 (ebook from Project Gutenberg, 2011).

Schneider, Ena. *Ribbons of Steel: The Story of Northern Alberta Railways.* Calgary: Detselig Enterprises Ltd., 1989.

Smith, Philip. *The Treasure-Seekers: The Men Who Built Home Oil.* MacMillan of Canada, 1978.

Smuin, Joe. *Kettle Valley Railway Mileboards: A Historical Field Guide to the KVR.* North Kildonan Publications, 2003.

Webb, Melody. *Yukon: The Last Frontier.* Vancouver: UBC Press, 1985, 1993.

TELEPHONE INTERVIEWS

Kenneth Cuttle, interviewed by Mary Trainer, 2013.

Zoe McKnight, interviewed by Mary Trainer, 2015.

PERSONAL INTERVIEWS

Alexis Bowley, interviewed by Mary Trainer, 2013.

Brad Coates, interviewed by Mary Trainer, 2013.

Randy Manuel, interviewed by Mary Trainer, 2013.

Ron Restrick, interviewed by Mary Trainer, 2013.

Don Evans, interviewed by Brian Antonson, 2013.

Ray Matthews, interviewed by Brian Antonson, 2014.

MAGAZINES AND NEWSPAPER ARTICLES

British Colonist, various dates.

Classic Trains Magazine, Spring 2014.

Ottawa Citizen, November 22, 1958.

Nelson Daily News, various dates.

Penticton Herald, July 1, 1943.

Penticton Herald, July 29, 1958.

Penticton Herald, January 24, 1958.

Legion Magazine, May/June 2012, pp. 36–39. Knowles, Valerie. "Women's Work."

Vancouver Sun, West Coast News, June 3, 2013, p. A4. "Railway noise tops list of complaints."

Burnaby Today, February 14, 1983, p. 3. "Does Peat Bog Have a Secret Train?"

Vancouver Sun, November 8, 1956, p. 1

WEBSITES

A number of websites were consulted during the research of this book; the key ones related to modern-day rail routes, experiences, and museums are found in the "Western Canada Rail Experiences" section, on pages 193–94. The authors encourage readers to seek further information on the stories in this book by conducting a simple Internet search.

REPORTS AND STATEMENTS

Commission of Inquiry, Hinton Train Collision: report of the Commissioner, the Honourable Mr. Justice René P. Foisy. Edmonton, Alberta, 1986.

Statements taken from the inquest re the Farron explosion, October 31, 1924, Grand Forks, BC.

Statements taken from the inquest into the Farron explosion, November 5, 1924, Nelson, BC.

Calgary Heritage Park's CPR 2024 provides nostalgia for some and an introduction to steam trains for others. **CALGARY HERITAGE PARK**

ACKNOWLEDGEMENTS

AS CO-AUTHORS, WE'VE benefitted from the help of many "friends of our book" as it came together along the journey through research, writing and production. We thank these people and institutions for their encouragement, professionalism, support, and belief in the book's merit.

Herb Dixon, Don Evans, Mike Harcourt, and Don Waite lent their names and words to endorse the book at manuscript stage, as did Harry Home, the Honourable Ione J. Christensen, and Garry Marchant, and we tip our conductors' hats to them in appreciation.

Individuals accepted our request to read and review parts of or all of the drafted writing at various stages, providing cogent, insightful comments and guidance, ever improving the work. Among those who strengthened our approach in this way are Fred Braches and Don Waite. We especially thank Harry Home and Ray Matthews. To Joe Smuin goes our gratitude for reviewing the manuscript and sharing his vast knowledge of railway history with us throughout the editorial process.

Railroad memories from Clif Chapman, Brad Coates, Kenneth Cuttle, Bruce Harvey, Ted Logie, Ray Matthews, Zoe McKnight, Jim Munsey, Ron Restrick, Joe Smuin, and David Watts greatly widened our range of topics.

Motivating us in a variety of crucial ways have been Alex Bowley, Earle Gray, Alvin and Anne Logie, David Mallory, Randy Manuel, Margaret McCuaig, Georgina Palm, Barrie Sanford, and Clinton Tippett.

A book with stories referencing over fifty locations needed a superb map to give readers context, and Eric Leinberger made that happen. For the two cover photographs, we are highly appreciative of the photography and artistic approach of Robert Bittner of Revelstoke. And for many of the interior photographs, we thank Don Waite for his professional improvements to our sourced work.

Seeing this book from concept to publication took the decision and vision of publisher Rodger Touchie and guidance from wordsmith editors Karla Decker and Lara Kordic. The beautiful cover design by Jacqui Thomas well reflected our own ambitions for the book.

Digging deep into archives is part of what amateur historians do, all the better when enabled by institutions that know where to direct us. We thank the BC Forest Discovery Centre, BC Archives, Kettle Valley Steam Railway, Mission Archives, Penticton Museum & Archives, and the Summerland Public Library.

Secluded time away from family is the essence of a writer's life and those who kept us happily tethered to the truer priorities of life include our partners: Mary's Neil, Brian's Sue, and Rick's Janice.

To the many others who knowingly or unknowingly nudged along this volume, we welcome you onboard and thank you for spending time with our book.

INDEX

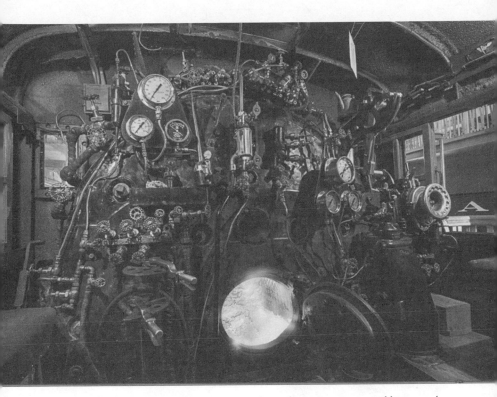

The cab of CP locomotive 5468 is a stunning and complex environment, capably managed by professional crews. **ROBERT BITTNER, PHOTOGRAPHER, REVYBAWB70@ME.COM**

ABOUT THE AUTHORS

INSPIRED BY BC historian Bill Barlee, who excelled at bringing British Columbia history alive for readers, Mary, Brian, and Rick researched and wrote *Slumach's Gold: In Search of a Legend* in 1972. Thirty-five years later, they updated the tale with new information and fresh insights; both editions became Canadian bestsellers and chosen for *The Essentials: 150 Great BC Books & Authors*, by Alan Twigg. The trio formed a publishing company, Nunaga Publishing, the name taken from an Inuit word meaning "My land, my country." During the next six years, Nunaga published over twenty books by a range of respected authors. Nunaga also published the magazine *Canadian Frontier*. The company was sold to Douglas & McIntyre in 1978.

MARY TRAINER

Mary has been writing about BC's people, places, and history for more than forty years. Her articles have been published in numerous newspapers, magazines, and historical journals. After a career in communications with Simon Fraser University and Metro Vancouver, she now lives in Summerland, BC, where she continues her passion for cycling, and serves on several community boards in the South Okanagan.

BRIAN ANTONSON

Brian retired from an active career in radio and broadcast education in 2010 and has since dedicated his time to travel, community

Authors Rick Antonson, Mary Trainer, and Brian Antonson at Engine 374 Pavilion, Roundhouse Community Arts and Recreation Centre, Vancouver. PHOTO BY NEIL TRAINER

service, and things that capture his fancy, including intriguing people, trains, the historical persons behind the legends of King Arthur, Corvettes, kaleidoscopes, the night skies, and the Slumach Lost Creek Gold Mine legend.

RICK ANTONSON

Rick Antonson was vice-president of Rocky Mountaineer Railtours, CEO of Edmonton Tourism, and CEO of Tourism Vancouver, and represented BC and Yukon on the Canadian Tourism Commission. He and sons Brent and Sean have circumnavigated the Northern Hemisphere by train. He recently travelled on Australia's India-Pacific train with his wife, Janice. He is the author of the *New York Times*–acclaimed book, *Route 66 Still Kicks*.

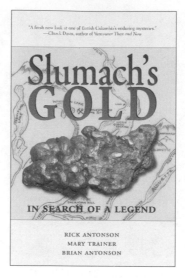

SLUMACH'S GOLD was a Canadian bestseller when it was first published in 1972, and so was its thirty-fifth-anniversary edition, which spent twenty-three weeks on the *Vancouver Sun*'s Top Ten Bestseller list when it was released in 2007. *Slumach's Gold: In Search of a Legend* greatly expands the original, bringing new research, fascinating updates, and fresh insights, chronicling what is possibly Canada's greatest lost-mine story. As of 2015, the 2007 version of *Slumach's Gold* has sold over 10,000 copies.

This book's story provides the background to the popular adventure series *The Curse of the Frozen Gold*, airing on History Channel and Animal Planet.